EINE PRISE HEIMAT

A PINCH OF HOME

Besonderer Dank an Carina Adam, Sabine Hueck - Atelier Culinário und
Grafikladen, ohne die das Buch nicht so schön geworden wäre!
Special thanks to Carina Adam, Sabine Hueck - Atelier Culinário and
Grafikladen without whom the book would not be so beautiful!

32

135

82

58

26

97

INHALT CONTENT

INHALT CONTENT

147

199

156

188

206

MY FUSION FOOD, OUR FUSION FOOD

Der Geruch ist der Sinn, der Zeitreisen ermöglicht. Ein vertrauter Duft und schon fühlen wir uns in eine andere Zeit katapultiert. Für geflüchtete Berlinerinnen und Berliner bestimmt häufig die Sehnsucht das Ziel dieser Reisen – zurück in die Vergangenheit, zurück in die Heimat. Aber Zeitreisen können auch in die Zukunft führen. So haben wir uns mit diesem Kochbuch das Ziel gesetzt, eine solche futuristische Reise zu unternehmen: Die Rezepte-Zeitmaschine befördert uns direkt in die Zukunft. Die Zukunft der Fusion Cuisine.

GESCHMACKS-FUSIONEN

Die Kombination von Esstraditionen, Kochkünsten und -techniken, Geschmacksrichtungen und grundlegenden Zutaten verschiedener kultureller und kulinarischer Prägung in einem einzigen Gericht wird als Food Fusion verstanden. Mit der Küche der geflüchteten Menschen gewinnt Food Fusion in Deutschland momentan eine neue Dynamik. Wo fusioniert wird, da gibt es allerdings auch Vorbehalte. So wurde Food Fusion gelegentlich als „Konfusionsküche" betitelt. Trotz solcher Vorbehalte hat sich die Fusion Cuisine weltweit durchgesetzt. Wir glauben, dass die Beiträge der zu uns geflüchteten Menschen unsere gesellschaftliche Wirklichkeit bereichern werden, ganz sicher auch auf kulinarischem Gebiet. Die in diesem Buch präsentierten Rezepte sprechen mit ihrer Köstlichkeit für sich selbst. Schließlich lässt sich auch fragen, welche Küche denn jemals frei von Einflüssen und Fusionen gewesen ist?

DAS BUCH UND SEINE GESCHICHTE

Das letzte Kochbuch von *Über den Tellerrand* liegt nun anderthalb Jahre zurück und inzwischen sind viele neue Rezepte einer gelebten Fusionsküche entstanden, die wir gerne teilen möchten. Bei der Auswahl der professionellen Köche für die Begegnungen in diesem Buch sind wir dann spontan vorgegangen. Da Spitzenköche eine sehr beschäftigte Berufsgruppe sind, haben wir im Laufe der Monate viele Köche kontaktiert und für unser Projekt geworben. Wir sind froh, dass so viele Bereitschaft gezeigt haben, kreativ wurden, sich Zeit für Vorgespräche und das gemeinsame Kochen genommen haben.

Während der Begegnungen von Sterneköchen und geflüchteten Kochbegeisterten stand nicht der Wissensaustausch im Vordergrund, sondern der Dialog. Auch das soll sich in den begleitenden Texten zu den Rezepten widerspiegeln. Die Auswahl der Rezepte haben wir dabei ganz den Kochenden überlassen. Als Ausgangspunkt bei der Rezeptentwicklung dienten Fragen rund um den Begriff der Heimat: Was erinnert dich besonders an Zuhause? Hast du eine Lieblingsspeise? Was ist deine ganz persönliche Prise Heimat? Das Ergebnis ist eine große Vielfalt, die sich unter dem Begriff der Fusion Cuisine zusammenfassen lässt. Jedes Rezept haben wir mehrmals nachgekocht, sodass die Fusion auch in den heimischen Küchen gelingen wird.

FOOD OF DREAMS

Oft steht am Anfang einer neuen kulinarischen Kreation ein Traum: Gerichte, von denen wir träumen, die wir nicht kennen, aber uns so genau ausmalen, dass uns beim Aufwachen das Wasser im Mund zusammenläuft. Food of Dreams. Solche kulinarischen Träume sind Anlässe für großartige, neue Gerichte. Wir wünschen uns, dass alle in unserer Gesellschaft mitmachen, Neues wagen, sich auf Experimente mit ungewissem Ausgang einlassen, ganz auf die Macht der Träume und das Potential der Neugier vertrauen.

In diesem Sinne wünschen wir viel Freude und Inspiration bei den hier gesammelten Beispielen gelebter Fusionsküche.

GEBRAUCHSANLEITUNG

– Alle Zutaten werden vor der Zubereitung gründlich gewaschen und geputzt.
– Pfeffer aus der Mühle und Meersalz verwenden.
– Obst und Gemüse in Bio-Qualität nutzen.
– Vegetarische Gerichte sind mit ⓥ gekennzeichnet.
– Anstatt mit einem Bunsenbrenner kann man die Zutaten auch im Ofen versengen.

Bei jedem Rezept findet ihr Angaben dazu, für wie viele Personen das Rezept ausgelegt ist und ob es sich um ein vegetarisches Gericht handelt. Bitte achtet darauf, ob die Mengenangaben für Vor- oder Hauptspeisen gemacht wurden. Lasst es euch schmecken und

#maketheworldabetterplate!

MY FUSION FOOD, OUR FUSION FOOD

Our sense of smell allows us to travel through time. A particularly familiar scent can instantly trigger a memory and transport us back to a moment in our past. This is also the case for many refugees in Berlin, for whom scents trigger an intense longing, a yearning for their pasts and for their homelands. However, traveling through time also opens the door to the future. With this cookbook, we aim to go on a journey through time, and the "recipe-time machine" will transport us directly to the future of fusion cuisine.

FUSION FLAVORS

Fusion cuisine is the combination of eating traditions, cooking techniques, flavors and ingredients from various culinary cultures, all in one single dish. Right now, with the diverse culinary traditions being brought into Germany with the refugees, fusion cuisine is gaining momentum. But where there is "fusion" there is often also skepticism. That is why fusion food is sometimes called confusion food. Despite this however, fusion cuisine is enjoyed by ever more people: not only in Germany, but also across the globe. We, from *Über den Tellerrand*, believe that the contributions made by the refugees enrich our society and in particular our culinary practices. The delicious recipes presented in this book speak for themselves... And ultimately we ask ourselves: which cuisine was ever free of foreign influences and fusions?

THE BOOK AND ITS STORY

It has now been one and a half years since the last *Über den Tellerrand* cookbook was published. In the meantime, many new recipes were created, which both the chefs and we would like to share with you. In choosing the professional chefs for the encounters in this book, we took a spontaneous approach. As being a professional chef tends to be a very busy profession, we contacted many of them over the past months and advertised our project. We are very pleased that so many of them were eager to work with us, were creative and took time for the preparations and cooking encounters. Following *Über den Tellerrand*'s philosophy, this cookbook is not just a collection of recipes for those who love good food and are enthusiastic cooks. It is also about sharing personal memories, and anecdotes about cooking and eating together. A combination of local ingredients and ingredients from far away countries is what makes our dishes so special and unique.

The focus of the encounters between the star chefs and our enthusiastic refugee chefs was not on the exchange of knowledge but rather on dialogue, which is reflected in the texts accompanying the recipes. The selection of recipes was left entirely to the chefs. We merely provided them with questions about "home" as a starting point: What reminds you of home? What is your favorite meal? What ingredient epitomises home to you? The results were incredibly diverse and they all came together in our "fusion cuisine".

THE FOOD OF DREAMS

Any new culinary creation starts with a dream: combined flavors that we may not have yet tasted, but that we imagine and savor so vividly, awaken our appetite. And these culinary dreams are occasions for wonderful new creations.

We encourage everyone in society to take part in such creations, to experiment and try out new things. Even when you do not know what you will create. Our wish for everyone is to harness the power of your dreams and the potential of your curiosity.

We invite you on an inspiring and enjoyable journey with our fusion cuisine recipes and the stories that come with them.

DIRECTIONS

– All ingredients need to be thoroughly cleaned and washed before preparation.
– Pepper from the mill and sea salt should be used for seasoning.
– Organic fruit and vegetables should be used when possible.
– Vegetarian dishes are labelled with (v)
– Insead of using a Bunsen burner, one can sear the ingredients in the oven.

Each recipe includes details on the amount of portions and whether it is vegetarian. Please be sure whether the quantities were made for starters or main dishes. Enjoy your meal and

#maketheworldabetterplate!

EINE PRISE HEIMAT

Jetzt ist es soweit – die Reise kann endlich losgehen. In diesem Kochbuch reisen wir kreuz und quer durch die Welt, von Ägypten bis Peru, von Syrien nach Gambia. Im Gespräch mit einem pakistanischen Koch stellen wir die Gemeinsamkeiten mit der indischen kulinarischen Tradition fest, die Österreicher lassen sich von Ungarn, Böhmen und Norditalien inspirieren und wer aus Peru oder Brasilien kommt, kennt sich häufig auch mit japanischen Kochkünsten gut aus. Doch obwohl uns heute viele Küchen und Geschmäcker von Reisen und Restaurantbesuchen bekannt sind – es gibt noch viel zu entdecken. Im Folgenden eine kleine bescheidene Einführung zu den vielfältigen und reichhaltigen Küchentraditionen, die unseren Gerichten eine Prise Heimat beigesteuert haben.

FOUL UND TAAMIYYA AUS ÄGYPTEN

Schon beim Frühstück beginnt die ägyptische Küche mit traditionellen und sehr landestypischen Gerichten: Foul und Taamiyya. Foul ist ein dicker Brei aus eingekochten Saubohnen, der mit Sesam, Zitrone, verschiedenen

Gewürzen und Öl verfeinert wird. Taamiyya sind frittierte Gemüsebällchen, die Falafeln ähneln. Hat man das Frühstück erledigt, kann man sich mit Mezze über den weiteren Tag retten. Mezze sind kleine Nebengerichte wie z.B. Hummus, ein Kichererbsenpüree, oder Baba Ghanoush, eine Auberginenpaste. Zu allen Speisen gehört Fladenbrot, das die Ägypter Aish bzw. „Leben" nennen. Gegen späten Abend kann man sich dann den Fleischgerichten widmen. Fleisch wird als Kebab, Kufta oder Hähnchen auf Holzkohle gegrillt. Typisch für Oberägypten sind die Tagine, Fleisch-Gemüse-Töpfe aus dem Ofen.

AFGHANISTAN AN DER SEIDENSTRASSE

Afghanistan liegt an der ehemals bedeutsamen Seidenstraße; das Netz der Karawanenstraßen hat zu einem intensiven Austausch in der Region beigetragen, der sich bis heute in der afghanischen Küche zeigt. Türkische, persische und indische Einflüsse lassen sich kulinarisch ausmachen. Innerhalb Afghanistans gibt es weitere regionale und ethnische Unterschiede, die sich in den Gerichten zeigen. Das wichtigste Grundnahrungsmittel ist jedoch stets Brot, hergestellt vor allem aus Weizenmehl. Aus lang-

körnigem Reis werden verschiedene Pilaws zubereitet, darunter Kabuli palaw, das Nationalgericht des Landes. Die bevorzugte Fleischsorte ist Lammfleisch, das auch häufig zu Kebab verarbeitet wird. Das wichtigste Milchprodukt ist Joghurt, der sehr oft verwendet wird. Den Abschluss einer Mahlzeit bildet oft Obst, am häufigsten Trauben und Melonen.

FISH CAKES AUS GAMBIA

Das westafrikanische Gambia ist in seiner Küche beeinflusst von der nordafrikanischen bzw. arabischen Küche. Grundnahrungsmittel der Küche Gambias bilden frische und getrocknete Fische sowie Reis, Süßkartoffeln, Maniok, Okra und anderes Gemüse. Erdnusssauce begleitet nahezu jedes Gericht der gambischen Küche. Typische Spezialitäten sind u.a. Sissay Yassa (in Zitronensaft mariniertes Hähnchen mit Zwiebeln und Ingwer), Benachin (Reisgericht aus Gemüse und getrocknetem Fisch) und Domoda (Eintopf mit Fleisch, Gemüse und der obligatorischen Erdnusssauce). Fish Cakes, mit Fisch gefüllte und kräftig gewürzte, frittierte Teigtaschen, sind ein verbreiteter Snack. Nach- und Süßspeisen sind dagegen kaum üblich in Gambia.

DIE SAHELKÜCHE DES NIGER

Die Küche des Nigers wird der traditionellen Sahelküche zugerechnet, die auch in den Nachbarländern Libyen, Nigeria, Tschad und Algerien verbreitet ist. Sie ist im Allgemeinen eher einfach-ländlich und meistens sehr scharf und würzig. Grundnahrungsmittel sind Reis, Mais und Bohnen. Viele Gerichte bestehen aus Reis und einer Fleisch-, Fisch- oder Gemüsesauce. Ein typisches Gericht der nigrischen Küche ist kolkoti und kofois (Maisgrütze mit einer Sauce aus Affenbrotbaumblättern).

MAXIMALE SÜSSE – DESSERTS AUS PAKISTAN

Die Küche Pakistans ist eng mit der nordindischen Küche verwandt, jedoch regional sehr unterschiedlich und vielfältig. Curries aus Gemüse wie Blumenkohl, Aubergine, Okra, Kartoffeln, Steckrüben oder Spinat mit und ohne Fleisch sind die typischsten Alltagsgerichte in Pakistan. Außerdem werden viel Hülsenfrüchte, vor allem Linsen, gegessen. Alle Gerichte ohne Reisbeilage werden mit Brot serviert. Das Brot gibt es in unterschiedlichen Sorten wie Tschapati (dünnes rundes Fladenbrot), Naan (rundes Fladenbrot aus Hefeteig), Taftan (Fladenbrot aus Hefe-

teig, mit Safran und Kardamom gewürzt) etc. Neben Curries sind Kebabs wichtiger Bestandteil der pakistanischen Küche. Süße Desserts wie Kulfi (gefrorene Milch mit Pistazien, Safran oder Kardamom), Kheer (süßer Reispudding) u.a. schließen ein pakistanisches Essen ab.

DER KULINARISCHE RUF SYRIENS

Die syrische Küche ist sehr vielfältig, aromatisch und raffiniert und gilt als eine der besten Küchen des Nahen Ostens. Sie ist nicht nur von der arabischen Küche, sondern auch von der französischen, jüdischen und türkischen Küche beeinflusst. Hauptzutaten der syrischen Küche sind vor allem Weizen, Kichererbsen, Oliven, Tomaten, Aprikosen, Granatäpfel, Datteln und Feigen und als Kräuter und Gewürze Minze, Kardamom, Zimt, Safran, Sesam und Kreuzkümmel. Als Fleisch wird hauptsächlich Lamm und Geflügel verzehrt, an der Küste auch viel Fisch und Meeresfrüchte. Wie auch in Ägypten und anderen Küchen des Orients bilden in der Küche Syriens die Mezze genannten Vorspeisen einen wichtigen Bestandteil eines typischen Essens. Abgeschlossen wird die Mahlzeit in Syrien gerne mit frischem Obst oder arabischem Süßgebäck aus Honig, Nüssen und Rosinen.

A PINCH
OF HOME

Let the journey begin! In this cookbook we will travel across the world, from Egypt to Peru, from Syria to Gambia, from Austria to Afghanistan. When speaking with a Pakistani chef we find similarities with culinary traditions from India, Austrians are inspired by Hungary, Bohemia and Northern Italy, and those who come from Peru or Brazil are often familiar with the great variety of Japanese cuisine. Even though we might be familiar with many cuisines and tastes - from eating in restaurants or traveling - there is still much to be discovered. Below, you will find a small and modest introduction to the richness of culinary traditions that have contributed a "pinch of home" to our dishes.

FOUL UND TAAMIYYA
FROM EGYPT

When they wake up, Egyptians start their day with very typical and traditional dishes: foul and taamiyya. Foul is a thick mash made of boiled beans and flavored with sesame, lemon, various spices and oil. Taamiyya are fried vegetable balls, similar to falafel. As soon as breakfast is finished, you make your way through the day with a great variety of mezze. Mezze are small side dishes such as hummus, a chickpea puree, or baba ghanoush, an eggplant paste. Every dish is commonly accompanied by flatbread, which is called aish or "life" in Egyptian. The late evening is devoted to meaty dishes: charcoal-grilled kebab, kufta or chicken are often on the menu. Typical in Upper Egypt are also tagine: meat and vegetable pots out of the oven.

AFGHANISTAN AND
THE SILK ROAD

Afghanistan lies on the ancient Silk Road, a network of caravan trading routes which enabled an intensive exchange in the region and highly influenced contemporary Afghan cuisine. Turkish, Persian as well as Indian influences are all present in the country's cuisine. But even within Afghanistan itself, there are regional and ethnic differences which are reflected in a great variety of dishes. However, the most important staple food is bread, made mainly from wheat flour. A variety of pilaus are prepared from long grain rice, including kabuli palau, the national dish of the country. The preferred type of meat is lamb, which is often served as kebab. A meal is usually topped off with fresh fruit – mostly grapes and melons.

FISH CAKES FROM GAMBIA

Located in West Africa, Gambia's cuisine is highly influenced by North African and Arab cuisine. The basic components of Gambian meals are fresh and dried fish as well as rice, sweet potatoes, cassava, okra and other vegetables. Peanut sauce accompanies almost every meal. Typical specialties are sissay yassa (chicken marinated in lemon with onions and ginger), jollof rice (a rice dish made from vegetables and dried fish) and domoda (a stew with meat, vegetables and the obligatory peanut sauce). Fish cakes, flavored fried dumplings stuffed with fish, are a common snack. However, sweets and desserts are not popular in Gambia.

NIGERIAN SAHEL
CUISINE

The Republic of Niger derives its flavors and dishes from the traditional Sahel cuisine, which has also influenced its neighbouring countries Libya, Nigeria, Chad and Algeria. Dishes are generally simple and mostly very hot and spicy. Rice, corn and beans are the basic ingredients of every meal. Many dishes consist of rice with a meat, fish or vegetable sauce. A typical dish in Nigerian cuisine is Kolkoti and Kofois (grits with a sauce made from baobab leaves).

MAXIMUM SWEETNESS–
DESSERTS
FROM PAKISTAN

While Pakistan's cuisine is closely related to that of Northern India, it is characterized by a great diversity and variety. Curries made from vegetables such as cauliflower, eggplant, okra, potatoes, turnips or spinach, with or without meat, are the most typical dishes of everyday life in Pakistan. Pulses, especially lentils, are also very common. All dishes without rice are served with bread. The bread comes in different varieties like chapati (thin round flat bread), naan (round flatbread made of yeast dough), taftan (flatbread made of yeast dough, flavored with saffron and cardamom) and many more. Besides curries, kebabs also play an important role in Pakistani cuisine. Sweet desserts such as kulfi (frozen milk with pistachios, saffron or cardamom) or kheer (sweet rice pudding), top off every meal.

THE CULINARY REPUTA-
TION OF SYRIA

Syrian cuisine is diverse, aromatic and refined, and is considered one of the best cuisines in the Middle East. It is not only influenced by Arabic cuisine, but also by the French, Jewish and Turkish cuisines. Its main ingredients are wheat, chickpeas, olives, tomatoes, apricots, pomegranates, dates, figs and spices such as mint, cardamon, cinnamon, saffron, sesame and cumin. Lamb and chicken are the most common types of meat and on the coast there is an abundance of seafood. Like in Egypt and other oriental cuisines, mezze, being the starters, are an important part of every traditional meal. A meal is usually concluded with fresh fruits or Arabic sweets made of honey, nuts and raisins.

1

WAS KOCHEN MIT LIEBE ZU TUN HAT: EIN AFGHANISCH-DEUTSCHES MÄRCHEN

WHY LOVE AND COOKING GO TOGETHER: AN AFGHAN-GERMAN FAIRY TALE

REZA & MICHAEL

Beim leidenschaftlichen Kochen läuft es mitunter wie in der Liebe: Gegensätze ziehen sich an. Weich und knusprig, sattes Gelb und frisches Grün, deutsche und persische Küche. Im Spiel mit den sogenannten Gegensätzen stellen sich diese häufig als ziemlich gute Kombinationen heraus. Reza und Michael haben während ihrer vergnügten Kochbegegnung so manchen Kontrast mit Meisterhand in wundervolle Gerichte umgesetzt: Linsensuppe mit Ei, Kartoffeln, Reis und Okra und als Nachtisch einen Safran-Limetten-Pudding. Mehrere Köche verderben den Brei? Nicht hier und auch beim Würzen heißt die Devise Vielzahl. Reza zeigt sich etwas belustigt hinsichtlich der deutschen Vorliebe für Salz, denn es gebe doch so viel mehr. Die Scheu vor dem Zuviel an Gewürz abzulegen, das lernt man aus der Begegnung mit der Küche seiner afghanischen Heimat. Michael lässt Regeln und Vorbehalte sowieso nicht gelten und folgt bei seinen Kochkünsten vielmehr dem Gefühl und der Lust am Experimentieren. Die Gegensätze etwa in den Farben wirken dabei auch in der Präsentation der Speisen vorteilhaft. Wer ein solches Essen dann genießt, schmackhaft und dazu noch so schön, der kann vor lauter Freude am Dasein richtig alt werden. Rezas Großvater ist genau so 145 Jahre alt geworden. Wer das nicht glauben kann, muss entweder unsere Rezepte selber testen – viele Jahrzehnte lang – oder er fragt Reza persönlich. Der arbeitet als Schuhmacher in den Hackeschen Höfen in Berlin und freut sich über Besuch. Die Moral von der Geschichte: Mit Leidenschaft kocht man, liebt man, erzählt man, und zwar überall.

Sometimes passionate cooking can be a lot like love: opposites attract. Smooth and crisp textures, deep yellows and fresh greens, German and Persian cuisine: the interplay of these apparent opposites brings up some pretty good combinations. During their cheerful cooking encounter, Reza and Michael skillfully transformed contrasts into wonderful dishes: lentil soup with egg, potatoes, rice and okra as well as a saffron and lime pudding for dessert. Multiple cooks spoil the broth? Not in this case. And as for seasoning the order of the day, too, is multitude. Reza seems amused by the Germans' fondness of salt, because there is a whole world of seasoning outside it. Putting aside the fear of adding too many spices is the first lesson learned from the encounter with the cuisine of his Afghan homeland. Michael, in any case, is not fazed by rules or restrictions and prefers to follow his instincts and desire to experiment when cooking. The contrasts in color for example are also advantageous for the presentation of the dishes. Whoever enjoys this food, delicious as it is beautiful, will grow to be very old indeed, purely by finding such joy in its existence. This is how Reza's grandfather turned exactly 145 years old. And if you don't believe it you should give our recipes a try, for a couple of decades at least, or ask Reza about it yourself. He works as a shoemaker at Hackesche Höfe in Berlin and would be delighted to see you. The moral of the story is: there is passion in cooking, loving, and telling stories – no matter where in the world.

MENÜ

FÜR 4 PERSONEN

VORSPEISE

LINSENVARIATIONEN AN POCHIERTEM EI

HAUPTSPEISE

KARTOFFEL-REIS-KUCHEN MIT FEINEN OKRASCHOTEN

NACHSPEISE

SAFRAN-LIMETTEN-CREME

LINSENVARIATIONEN
AN POCHIERTEM EI
500 g rote Linsen

Für die Linsensuppe:
1 Zwiebel
2 Knoblauchzehen
400 g geschälte Tomaten
1 l Wasser
2 – 3 TL Salz
1/2 TL Pfeffer
1 1/2 TL Currypulver

Für den Linsensalat:
1 Zwiebel
3 Karotten
5 g frischer Koriander
10 g frische Minze
10 g frischer Ingwer
1 Zitrone
2 EL Rapsöl
2 EL Weißweinessig

Für das pochierte Ei:
4 Eier
Zucker

Zum Anrichten:
50 g Wildreis
Rapsöl zum Frittieren

KARTOFFEL-REIS-
KUCHEN MIT FEINEN
OKRASCHOTEN
Für den Kartoffel-Reis-Kuchen:
300 g Basmatireis
3 große Kartoffeln
1 g Safranfäden
1 Ei

Für die Okraschoten:
400 g Okraschoten
5 Knoblauchzehen
3 EL Pflanzenöl
Salz

Zum Anrichten:
2 EL Sauerrahm
1 Prise Kreuzkümmelsamen

SAFRAN-
LIMETTEN-CREME
800 ml Milch
5 EL Reismehl
1 1/2 EL Zucker
1 1/2 EL Honig
2 EL Pistazien
0,5 g Safranfäden
100 ml Rosenwasser oder
Orangenblütenwasser

Zum Anrichten:
2 Limetten
Zucker
2 EL Pistazien,
in der Pfanne geröstet
2 EL essbare Blüten
(z.B.: Eisbegonien, Veilchen, ...)
1 EL Wildkräuter
(z.B.: Schafgarbe,
Sauerklee, Wiesenkerbel,...)
1 TL rosa Pfefferbeeren

DELICIOUS LENTIL VARIATION ON POACHED EGG

500 g red lentils

For the lentil soup:
1 onion
2 garlic cloves
400 g peeled tomatoes
1 l water
2–3 tsp. salt
1/2 tsp. pepper
1 1/2 tsp. curry powder

For the lentil salad:
1 onion
3 carrots
5 g fresh coriander
10 g fresh mint
10 g fresh ginger
1 lemon
2 Tbsp. canola oil
2 Tbsp. white vinegar

For the poached egg:
4 eggs
sugar

POTATO-RICE CAKE WITH DELICATE OKRAS

For the puffed wild rice:
50 g wild rice
canola oil for frying

For the potato-rice cake:
300 g basmati rice
3 potatoes
1 g saffron threads
1 egg

For the okras:
400 g okras
5 garlic cloves
3 Tbsp. vegetable oil
salt

For serving:
2 Tbsp. sour cream
cumin seeds

SAFFRON-LIME CREAM

800 ml milk
5 tbsp. rice flour
1 1/2 Tbsp. sugar
1 1/2 Tbsp. honey
2 Tbsp. pistachios
1–2 g saffron threads
100 ml rosewater or orange flower water

For serving:
2 limes
sugar
2 Tbsp. roasted pistachios
2 Tbsp. edible flowers (e.g. violets, squash flowers, ...)
1 Tbsp. weeds (e.g. yarrow, sorrel, cow parsley, ...)
1 tsp. pink pepper berries

MENUE
SERVES 4

STARTER

LENTIL VARIATION ON POACHED EGG

MAIN DISH

POTATO-RICE CAKE WITH DELICATE OKRAS

DESSERT

SAFFRON-LIME CREAM

LINSENVARIATIONEN AN POCHIERTEM EI
LENTIL VARIATION ON POACHED EGG

LINSEN

Die Linsen waschen und ca. 15 Minuten in 1 l Wasser vorkochen, dann in einem Sieb abtropfen lassen. 3/5 der Linsen für die Linsensuppe bereitstellen und 2/5 für den Salat.

LINSENSUPPE

Die Zwiebel in Würfel schneiden und andünsten. Den Knoblauch hacken und hinzugeben. Im Anschluss die Linsen kurz mitdünsten und dann die geschälten Tomaten unterrühren. Das Wasser hinzufügen und das Ganze für 20 Minuten kochen lassen. Mit Salz, Pfeffer und Curry abschmecken, pürieren und am Schluss durch ein feines Sieb passieren.

LINSENSALAT

Die Zwiebel in feine Würfel schneiden und kurz in kochendem Wasser blanchieren. Das nimmt der Zwiebel den kräftigen Geschmack. Währenddessen die Karotten in sehr feine Würfel schneiden, die Kräuter sehr fein hacken, die Zitronenschale fein abreiben und die Frucht entsaften. Zwiebel, Karotten und Linsen in eine Schale geben und geriebene Zitronenzeste hinzufügen. Den Ingwer reiben und ebenfalls hinzugeben. Mit etwas Öl, Essig und dem Saft einer Zitrone marinieren, einige Minuten ziehen lassen und zum Schluss die Kräuter hinzugeben.

POCHIERTES EI

Die Eier einzeln in eine Schale schlagen und in kochendes Wasser geben. Dafür das Wasser zuvor stark umrühren und dann jedes Ei einzeln vom äußeren Rand in das Wasser gleiten lassen. Ca. 5 Minuten im Wasser knapp unter dem Siedepunkt ziehen lassen. Das Ei danach mit etwas Zucker und einem Bunsenbrenner karamellisieren.

ZUM ANRICHTEN

Öl in einem Topf auf 180°C erhitzen und den Wildreis frittieren, bis er aufpufft. Mit einem Metallsieb herausnehmen und zum Entfetten auf Küchenpapier legen. In kleinen Schüsseln die Linsensuppe an dem Linsensalat und den porchierten Eiern anrichten und den gepufften Wildreis darüberstreuen.

LENTILS

Wash the lentils and precook them for about 15 minutes in 1 l water. Drain with a strainer. Keep 3/5 for the lentil soup and 2/5 for the salad.

LENTIL SOUP

Chop the onion and fry in a pan. Chop the garlic and fry together with the onion. Add the lentils and briefly fry everything together. Mix in the peeled tomatoes and the water and let cook for 20 minutes. Season with the spices, puree everything and pass through a strainer.

LENTIL SALAD

Chop the onion and briefly blanch in boiling water in order to decrease the strong onion taste. Meanwhile finely dice the carrots, chop the herbs, grate the lemon peel and juice the fruit. Place onion, carrots and lentils in a bowl and add grated lemon peel. Grate ginger and add to the mix as well. Marinate with oil, vinegar and the lemon juice, and let sit for a few minutes. Top with the freshly chopped herbs.

POACHED EGG

Crack the eggs each in a seperate bowl and pour in boiling water as followed: thoroughly stirr the water and then let one egg after another slide into the water from the outer edge of the pot. Allow to steep for 5 minutes right below boiling temperature. Sprinkle some sugar on top of the eggs and caramelize the eggs using a Bunsen burner.

FOR SERVING

Heat up oil in a pan to 180°C. Deep-fry wild rice in the hot oil until it is all puffed. Take the wild rice out of the oil by using a sieve and place on a paper towel to degrease. In a bowl, serve the soup with the salad and poached eggs and sprinkle the puffed wild rice over it.

24

1 Die Linsen vorkochen und abtropfen lassen. Cook and drain the lentils. 2 Die Karotten in sehr feine Würfel schneiden. Finely dice the carrots. 3 Die Zitronenschale fein abreiben. Finely grate the lemon peel. 4 Die Zitrone entsaften. Juice the lemon. 5 Den Ingwer in den Salat reiben. Grate the ginger and add to the salad. 6 Das pochierte Ei mit braunem Zucker karamellisieren. Caramelize the egg with brown sugar. 7 Die Suppe vor dem Servieren durch ein feines Sieb passieren. Pass soup through a strainer before serving.

KARTOFFEL-REIS-KUCHEN MIT FEINEN OKRASCHOTEN
POTATO-RICE CAKE WITH DELICATE OKRAS

KARTOFFEL-REIS-KUCHEN
Den Reis für ca. 5 Stunden in Wasser einweichen lassen und im Anschluss für 10 Minuten ohne Salz vorkochen, danach abseihen. Die Safranfäden in einem Mörser zerkleinern und über Nacht in 100 ml Wasser einweichen lassen — Die Kartoffeln schälen und in dünne Scheiben schneiden. Eine Pfanne mit Backpapier auslegen, die Kartoffelscheiben kreisförmig darauf platzieren und mit Öl bestreichen. Mit einem kleinen Gewicht beschwert von beiden Seiten langsam braten. Danach die Kartoffelsonne vom Backpapier befreien. — Den vorgekochten Reis mit Ei, Safran (inkl. Wasser) und etwas Salz vermengen und auf die Kartoffelsonne geben. Erneut mit Backpapier umwickeln und von beiden Seiten in der Pfanne durchgaren.

OKRASCHOTEN
Die Okraschoten in mundgroße Stücke schneiden. Den Knoblauch schälen, vierteln und danach mit den Okraschoten und 2 El Pflanzenöl in einer Pfanne scharf anbraten und mit Salz abschmecken.

ZUM ANRICHTEN
Den Kartoffel-Reis-Kuchen zusammen mit den Okraschoten auf einem Teller anrichten und mit etwas Sauerrahm und Kreuzkümmelsamen bestreut servieren.

POTATO-RICE CAKE
Soak the rice in water for about 5 hours, afterwards pre-cook it for 10 minutes in unsalted water and drain with a strainer. — Peel the potatoes, cut them into thin slices and arrange the raw potato slices in a circle between 2 baking sheets. Sprinkle everything with oil, place in a pan, weigh down (using e.g. another saucepan) and slowly cook through. — Mix the rice with the egg, saffron and salt. Take off the backing sheets, distribute this rice-saffron mix on the potato cake and cook thoroughly from both sides in a pan.

OKRAS
Cut okras into bite sized pieces. Peel the garlic and cut into quarters. — Heat up vegetable oil in a pan and sear okras and garlic. Season with salt.

FOR SERVING
Serve the potato-rice cake along with the okras and sprinkle with sour cream and some cumin seeds.

SAFRAN-LIMETTEN-CREME
SAFFRON-LIME CREAM

(V)

ZUBEREITUNG
Einen Tag zuvor die Safranfäden in 100 ml Rosen-
wasser einlegen. — Das
Reismehl mit ca. 200 ml
Milch mischen und für
15 Minuten ziehen las-
sen. Währenddessen die
Pistazien grob hacken.
— Die restliche Milch in
einem Topf erhitzen
und Zucker, Honig sowie
das Safran-Rosenwas-
ser hinzugeben. — Das
Reismehl-Milch-Ge-
misch in die heiße Milch
geben und 15 Minuten
köcheln lassen. Gelegent-
lich umrühren und ge-
gen Ende die Pistazien
hinzufügen. — Die Creme
in 6 kleine Förmchen
geben und im Kühlschrank
kalt stellen.

ZUM ANRICHTEN
Die 2 Limetten filetieren
und auf einem Küchen-
papier abtropfen lassen.
Dann mit etwas Zucker
bestreuen und mit einem
Bunsenbrenner karamel-
lisieren. — Die Pistazien
halbieren. Die Blüten
und Kräuter zupfen. — Die
karamellisierten Limet-
tenfilets auf der Creme verteilen (pro Förmchen
3 Filets). Anschließend
mit den Blüten, den
Kräutern und jeweils ca.
3 Pfefferbeeren pro
Schale garnieren.

PREPARATION
The day before, pickle
saffron threads in
100 ml rosewater. — Mix
rice flour with 200 ml
milk and allow to steep
over low heat for 15
minutes. Meanwhile chop
pistachios. — Heat up
the remaining milk along
with the sugar, honey
and saffron rosewater in
a saucepan. — Add the
rice flour milk mix to the
sweetened, heated milk
and let cook for 15 minutes,
stirring occasionally. At
the end of the cooking
process add pistachios.
— Pour the cream into
6 small forms and allow to
cool down in the fridge.

FOR SERVING
Slice the 2 limes and drain
well on a paper towel.
Sprinkle with sugar and
caramelize using a Bunsen
burner. — Chop up the
pistachios and pick flowers
and herbs. — Distribute
the caramelized lime fillets
on the cream (3 fillets
per form). Then garnish with
flowers, herbs and about
3 pepper berries each
ramekin.

REZA & MICHAEL

29

2

HARISSA,
ABER BITTE MIT SAHNE

HARISSA,
WITH CREAM PLEASE

MUDAR & ANDI

Der Ansatz des Kochteams Andreas und Mudar basiert auf der Idee, syrische Rezepte mit einer von der deutschen Sterneküche geprägten Handschrift zu übertragen. Fusion kann auch Übersetzung sein. So wird die Nachspeise, ein syrisches Grießküchlein bzw. Harissa, mit Sahne verfeinert, die hierzulande als Klassiker zum Kuchen gereicht wird. Geröstete Cashewkerne sorgen für eine weitere, nussige Geschmacksnote, geriebene Zitrone und Orange für die fruchtige Frische. Die Zubereitung der Hauptspeise, Lammschulter mit Essig und Zitronensäure, ist neu für Andreas, der sich von der Geschmacksvielfalt des Suds begeistert zeigt. Die intensiven aromatischen Geschmäcker der syrischen Küche sind eine Klasse für sich. Durch das filigrane Finish bei Anrichtung und Toppings perfektioniert Andreas jedes Gericht, ohne dieses jedoch im Kern zu verändern. Im Fall von Mudar und Andreas bedeutet Fusionsküche, das Beste aus beiden Kochwelten zu vereinen, überzusetzen in fremde Welten. Mit jedem Bissen schmeckt man den Spaß, den die beiden bei diesem kulinarischen Experiment hatten.

The approach chosen by the cooking team of Andreas and Mudar is to give Syrian recipes an exquisite note characterized by German gourmet cuisine. Fusion can also mean translation. In this vein, the dessert, a small Syrian semolina cake or harissa, is refined with cream, a basic ingredient of almost every German dessert. Roasted cashews are added for a nutty flavor, while grated lemon and orange zest make for a fruity freshness. Preparing the lamb shoulder for the main course with vinegar and citric acid is new for Andreas, who is fascinated by the variety of tastes in the stock. The intense aromas of Syrian cuisine are in a class of their own. Carefully refining the presentation and topping the dishes, Andreas adds the finishing touches, yet without changing them in their essence. Fusion means engaging with something new and, in Mudar's and Andreas' case, uniting the best from two worlds of cooking, ferrying to foreign lands. With every bite you can truly taste the fun both of the cooks had while preparing the meal.

MENÜ

VORSPEISE

GEBEIZTER LACHS AN PIKANTEM PAPRIKASUD

HAUPTSPEISE

HERZHAFTE SYRISCHE LAMMKEULE AUS DEM OFEN

NACHSPEISE

HARISSA KÜCHLEIN MIT ZITRUSNOTE

GEBEIZTER LACHS AN PIKANTEM PAPRIKASUD

Für den Lachs:
400 g Lachs in Sashimi-Qualität
100 g grobes Meersalz
100 g schwarze Pfefferkörner

Für den Paprikasud:
1 gelbe Paprika
1 rote Paprika
5 Knoblauchzehen
40 g brauner Zucker
30 ml weißer Balsamico
2 g Meersalz
20 Pfefferkörner
400 ml Wasser

Für die gebrannten Zwiebeln:
2 Zwiebeln
1 g Meersalz

Für die gebackenen Kartoffelwürfel:
2 Kartoffeln
1 l Rapsöl
Salz

Zum Anrichten:
1 Champignon
frische Minze

HERZHAFTE SYRISCHE LAMMKEULE AUS DEM OFEN

Für die Lammkeule:
1 Lammkeule (800 gr)
20 Knoblauchzehen
1 EL Kardamom
1/2 EL weißer Pfeffer
2 EL Meersalz
50 ml Weißweinessig
1 Zitrone
300 ml Wasser

Für den Reis:
300 g Basmatireis
ca. 800 ml Wasser
1 TL Kardamomkapseln
2 Zimtstangen
2 Lorbeerblätter
1 TL Kurkuma
1 Anisstern
1 TL schwarze Pfefferkörner
2 getrocknete Limetten
3 EL Pflanzenöl
1 EL Meersalz

Zum Anrichten:
3 EL Granatapfelkerne
1 EL fein geschnittene Korianderstiele
1 EL feine Korianderblätter
2 EL gehackte, rohe Mandeln

HARISSA KÜCHLEIN MIT ZITRUSNOTE

Für die Küchlein:
250 ml Wasser
200 g Zucker
500 g Hartweizengrieß
180 g Margarine
3 EL Naturjoghurt
1 Pkg. Backpulver
1 Pkg. Vanillezucker
1 TL Natron
1 Handvoll Cashewkerne

Zum Anrichten:
20 g Zucker
1 TL Rosenwasser
50 ml Wasser
250 ml Sahne
1 Zitrone
1 Orange

MARINATED SALMON IN ZESTY PEPPER STOCK

For the salmon:
400 g salmon, sashimi-quality
100 g coarse sea salt
100 g black peppercorns

For the pepper stock:
1 yellow bell pepper
1 red bell pepper
5 garlic cloves
40 g brown sugar
30 ml white balsamic vinegar
2 g sea salt
20 peppercorns
400 ml water

For the burnt onions:
2 onions
1 g sea salt

For the baked potato cubes:
2 potatoes
1 l rapeseed oil

For serving:
1 mushroom
fresh mint

SAVORY SYRIAN OVEN ROASTED LEG OF LAMB

For the leg of lamb:
1 leg of lamb (800 gr)
20 garlic cloves
1 Tbsp. cardamom
1/2 Tbsp. white pepper
2 Tbsp. sea salt
50 ml white vinegar
1 lemon
300 ml water

For the rice:
300 g basmati rice
800 ml water
1 tsp. cardamom capsules
2 cinnamon sticks
2 bay leaves
1 tsp. turmeric
1 star anise
1 tsp. black peppercorns
2 dried limes
3 Tbsp. vegetable oil
1 Tbsp. sea salt

For serving:
3 Tbsp. pomegranate seeds
1 Tbsp. finely chopped
coriander stalks
1 Tbsp. fine coriander leaves
2 Tbsp. chopped raw almonds

LITTLE HARISSA CAKES WITH CITRUS NOTES

For the cakes:
250 ml water
200 g sugar
500 g semolina
180 g margarine
3 Tbsp. plain yoghurt
1 pkg. baking powder
1 pkg. vanilla sugar
1 tsp. baking soda
1 handful of cashews

For serving:
20 g sugar
1 tsp. rosewater
50 ml water
250 ml cream
1 lemon
1 orange

MENUE
SERVES 4

STARTER

MARINATED SALMON IN ZESTY PEPPER STOCK

MAIN DISH

SAVORY SYRIAN OVEN ROASTED LEG OF LAMB

Ⓥ
DESSERT

LITTLE HARISSA CAKE WITH CITRUS NOTES

GEBEIZTER LACHS AN PIKANTEM PAPRIKASUD
MARINATED SALMON IN ZESTY PEPPER STOCK

LACHS
Die Pfefferkörner in einer Pfanne rösten, bis sie ihr volles Aroma entfalten. — Den gerösteten Pfeffer zusammen mit dem groben Meersalz in einem Mörser fein zermahlen und den Lachs von beiden Seiten mit der Mischung einreiben. — Nach 30 Minuten den Lachs von der Beize befreien, abspülen und trocken tupfen.

PAPRIKASUD
Die rote und gelbe Paprika mit einem Bunsenbrenner vorsichtig versengen, die Schale entfernen und klein schneiden. Die Knoblauchzehen zerdrücken und mit den klein geschnittenen Paprikas sowie den restlichen Zutaten in einen Topf geben. Den Sud langsam köchelnd auf ein Viertel einreduzieren. Im Anschluss alles pürieren und durch ein feines Sieb passieren.

GEBRANNTE ZWIEBELN
Die Haushaltszwiebeln schälen, aufschneiden und 5 Minuten warten, bis etwas Flüssigkeit ausgetreten ist. Die Schnittseite mit einem Bunsenbrenner versengen. — Danach etwas Meersalz darübergeben, in Alufolie wickeln, und 20 Minuten bei 130°C im Ofen garen. — Die abgekühlten Zwiebeln in ihre Segmente unterteilen und zum Anrichten bereitstellen.

GEBACKENE KARTOFFELWÜRFEL
Die Kartoffeln in kleine Würfel schneiden und in 130°C heißem Fett frittieren, bis diese weich sind. Die Kartoffelwürfel abtropfen lassen und das Fett auf 170°C erhitzen. — Die Kartoffeln goldgelb frittieren, bis keine Blasen mehr aufsteigen. Auf Küchenpapier entfetten und mit Salz würzen.

ZUM ANRICHTEN
Den Champignon mit der Mandoline in feine Scheiben schneiden. Die feinsten Blättchen der Minze pflücken. — Nun den Lachs in dünne Scheiben schneiden und auf einem Teller gemeinsam mit den Zwiebeln, den Champignonscheiben, den Kartoffelwürfeln und der Minze anrichten. Zum Schluss den Paprikasud darübergeben.

SALMON
Roast the peppercorns in a frying pan until they release their full flavor. — Grind roasted pepper and coarse sea salt in a mortar. — Rub the salt and pepper mixture on both sides of the salmon. After 30 minutes, remove marinade, wash and pat dry.

PEPPER STOCK
Char the red and yellow bell peppers using a Bunsen burner. After charring, peel and chop the peppers finely. Peel and crush the garlic, then mix it together with the chopped peppers and the remaining ingredients in a pot. Let the broth simmer slowly until it has boiled down to a quarter of its original volume. Afterwards, blend it and pass through a sieve.

ONIONS
Cut onions in half and wait for 5 minutes, or until some juice has leaked out. Char the cut surface with a Bunsen burner. — After charring, season with salt, wrap the onions in aluminium foil, and cook for 20 minutes in the oven at 130°C. — Segment the cooled onions into their natural layers and set aside for the final dish.

POTATO CUBES
Cube the potatoes and deep-fry them in 130°C hot oil until soft. — Drain the potato cubes and heat oil to 170°C. — Deep-fry the potatoes until they are golden and no more bubbles appear in the oil. Place them on paper towels to drain, and season with salt.

FOR SERVING
With a mandolin, slice the mushroom and pick out the freshest mint leaves. — Slice salmon thinly and arrange it together with onions, mushroom slices, potato cubes and mint leaves on a plate. Top everything with the pepper stock.

HERZHAFTE SYRISCHE LAMMKEULE AUS DEM OFEN
SAVORY SYRIAN OVEN ROASTED LEG OF LAMB

LAMMKEULE

Die 20 Knoblauchzehen schälen und zusammen mit Kardamom, Meersalz und dem weißen Pfeffer im Mörser zu einer Paste verarbeiten. — Die Zitrone auspressen und den Zitronensaft mit dem Weißweinessig zur Paste geben und zu einer Sauce verrühren. — Die Lammkeule ungefähr dreimal bis auf den Knochen einschneiden und in einem Bräter gut mit der Sauce marinieren. — Nun das Wasser hinzugießen und mit geschlossenem Deckel 3 Stunden bei 130°C im Ofen garen, bis sich das Fleisch leicht vom Knochen lösen lässt. Kurz vor dem Servieren bei Oberhitze goldbraun backen.

REIS

Außer den getrockneten Limetten, alle Gewürze mit einem Mörser fein zerreiben und in einem ausreichend großen Topf mit dem Öl anrösten, bis sich das volle Gewürzaroma entfaltet — Mit ca. 800 ml Wasser aufgießen und dann die getrockneten Limetten hinzugeben. — Den Basmatireis hinzufügen und auf mittlerer Flamme kochen, bis dieser gar ist.

ZUM ANRICHTEN

Den Reis zusammen mit dem Lammfleisch auf einem Teller anrichten und mit etwas Bratenfond beträufeln. — Zuletzt die Granatapfelkerne zusammen mit den Korianderstielen und den Mandeln darüber streuen. Den Bratenfond separat reichen.

LAMB

Grind peeled garlic cloves together with cardamom, sea salt and white pepper in a mortar until a paste forms. — Juice the lemon, mix with white vinegar and add to the paste in order to create a sauce. — Cut the leg of lamb about three times down to the bone, coat with sauce and place in a roasting pan. — Add water, cover the pan and cook for 3 hours in the oven at 130°C, until the meat comes off the bone easily. Right before serving, roast until golden brown with the oven's upper grill function.

RICE

Finely grind all spices except for the dried limes in a mortar. Roast the spices with oil in a large pot until they release their full flavor. — Add 800 ml water and the dried limes to the pot. — Add basmati rice and cook on medium heat until the rice is cooked.

FOR SERVING

Serve rice together with roasted lamb leg on one plate. Drizzle with lamb stock. — Top everything with pomegranate seeds, coriander and chopped almonds. Serve left-over lamb stock in a seperate bowl.

38

HARISSA KÜCHLEIN MIT ZITRUSNOTE
LITTLE HARISSA CAKE WITH CITRUS NOTES

KÜCHLEIN

Zuerst das Wasser und den Zucker zum Kochen bringen, die Margarine hinzugeben und schmelzen lassen. Mit den restlichen Zutaten (bis auf die Cashewkerne) zu einer homogenen Masse verrühren und auf einem Backblech verteilen. — Den Grießmix für ca. 1 Stunde im Kühlschrank ruhen lassen. — Danach mit etwas Margarine bepinseln, die Cashewkerne darauf verteilen und für ca. 25 Minuten bei 180°C (Unterhitze) backen. — Wenn sich der Rand langsam rötlich färbt, den Kuchen nochmals für 5 Minuten bei 180°C Oberhitze backen.

ZUM ANRICHTEN

Die Orangen- und Zitronenschale fein abreiben, dann die Orange und die Zitrone auspressen. Die Sahne steif schlagen. — Den Zucker zusammen mit dem Rosenwasser, dem Wasser sowie mit dem frisch gepressten Zitronen- und Orangensaft kurz aufkochen lassen und über den Kuchen träufeln, sodass sich dieser vollsaugt. — Den Kuchen in kleine Küchlein schneiden und mit der Sahne und etwas Orangen- und Zitronenzeste dekorieren.

CAKES

Bring water, sugar and semolina to the boil. — Mix in all remaining ingredients except for the cashews and spread on a baking pan. Allow to cool down for 1 hour in the refrigerator. — After the dough has settled, brush a little bit of margarine and sprinkle cashews on top and bake for 25 minutes in the oven at 180°C bottom heat. — When the edges turn red, bake for another 5 minutes at 180°C top heat.

FOR SERVING

Finely grate orange and lemon zest, then press orange and lemon for juice. Whip the cream with a handmixer until soft peaks form. — Bring the sugar, rosewater and water together with the lemon and orange juice to the boil, and drizzle over the cake until it becomes saturated with juice. — Cut into little cakes and decorate with whipped cream and some lemon and orange zest.

1 Lachsfilet in Sashimi Qualität. Sashimi-quality salmon fillet. 2 Den Lachs von beiden Seiten mit geröstetem Pfeffer und Meersalz einreiben. Rub salt and roasted pepper on both sides of the salmon. 3 Durch das Versengen erhält die Paprika einen leichten rauchigen Grillgeschmack. While charring, the pepper gets a slight smoky taste. 4 Den Paprikasud durch ein feines Sieb passieren. Strain the pepper stock through a sieve. 5 Die Zwiebeln an der Schnittstelle versengen. Char the cut surface of the onions. 6 Gebrannte Zwiebeln eignen sich für das Finish vieler Gerichte. Roasted onions are suitable for the finish of several dishes. 7 Die feinen Kartoffelwürfel in Öl frittieren. Fry the potato cubes in oil.

3

GENÜSSE AUS GAMBIA, VOLL VEGETARISCH

GAMBIAN INDULGENCES, COMPLETELY VEGETARIAN

MUSTAPHA & HOLGER

Holger aus Deutschland und Mustapha aus Gambia haben versucht, aus den Zutaten westafrikanischer traditioneller Gerichte etwas ganz Neues zu kreieren. Das Ergebnis: ein frischer Salat mit Erdnüssen, Mango und frittierten Auberginen, ein Eintopf aus schwarzen Linsen mit frischem Kokosnussfleisch und zum fulminanten Abschluss ein süßes Apfel-Mango-Risotto. Risotto, das war ganz neu für Mustapha, der in seinen zwei Jahren in Berlin bereits viel Koch- und Backerfahrungen gesammelt hat. Unter anderem in der Flüchtlingsbäckerei Bantabaa, in der er Neues ausprobieren kann und dabei sein kulinarisches Geschick unter Beweis stellen kann. In der Schärfe werden die traditionellen Rezepte dabei immer deutlich angepasst an den deutschen Gaumen. Wobei Mustapha überzeugt ist, dass viele Chilis – gerne die besonders scharfen Habaneros – in ihrer schweißtreibenden Wirkung zu Gesundheit und Schlankheit beitragen. Ein neuer Ansatz für eine Diät? Lieber nicht, bei uns geht es doch ganz und gar um den Genuss. *Hmm, adiata!* „Lecker" auf Mandika, Mustaphas Muttersprache. Das ist das Motto dieser köstlichen Gerichte!

Creating something completely new out of the ingredients of traditional West African cuisine? This was the challenge for Holger from Germany and Mustapha from Gambia. The result: a fresh salad with peanuts, mango and fried eggplants, a black lentil stew with fresh coconut flesh and as brilliant finish: a sweet mango-risotto. Risotto was something entirely new for Mustapha, who has already had the chance to gain a lot of cooking and baking experience during his two years in Berlin. For example, he regularly experiments with new creations in the refugee bakery Bantabaa, where he demonstrates his culinary skills. Although Mustapha is convinced that chili – especially the extra-spicy habaneros – enhance health and beauty in their sweat-inducing effect, his traditional recipes nonetheless usually need to be adapted to German taste buds. A new way of dieting? Not really, as with us everything is entirely about pleasure. *Hmm, adiata!* "Delicious" in Mandika, Mustapha's mother tongue, is the motto for our flavorful meals!

46

MENÜ

VORSPEISE

AROMATISCHER ERDNUSSSALAT

HAUPTSPEISE

BUNTER EINTOPF MIT SCHWARZEN LINSEN

NACHSPEISE

APFEL-MANGO-RISOTTO

AROMATISCHER ERDNUSSSALAT

100 g Erdnüsse
3 Paprika (rot, gelb, grün)
1 Aubergine
3 EL Kartoffelstärke
Pflanzenöl zum Frittieren
4 Limetten
1 Chili
2 Schalotten
10 g Ingwer
70 g Koriander
1 vollreife Mango
Sesamöl
Salz
Rohrzucker

BUNTER EINTOPF MIT SCHWARZEN LINSEN

50 g Sellerie
1 Süßkartoffel
2 Karotten
2 Zwiebeln
200 g schwarze Linsen
600 ml Gemüsefond
2 Knoblauchzehen
50 g Weißkraut
30 Kirschtomaten
2 1/2 Limetten
20 g Ingwer
1 Handvoll Koriander
1 Handvoll Thymian
1 Handvoll Petersillie
1 Handvoll Minze
100 g Kokosnussfleisch oder
Kokosflocken

Zum Anrichten:
4 EL Sauerrahm

APFEL-MANGO-RISOTTO

1 1/2 Äpfel
1 reife Mango
80 g Risottoreis
300 ml Kokosnussmilch
200 ml Wasser
120 g Rohrzucker
1 Orange
2 Zitronen
2 EL Honig
3 EL Kokosraspeln
Pflanzenöl

Zum Anrichten:
Kokosflocken
1 Handvoll frische Minze

AROMATIC PEANUT SALAD

100 g peanuts
3 bell peppers
(red, yellow, green)
1 eggplant
corn starch
oil for deep-frying
4 limes
1 chili
2 shallots
10 g ginger
70 g coriander
1/2 ripe mango
sesame oil
salt
cane sugar

BLACK LENTIL STEW

50 g celery
1 sweet potato
2 carrots
2 onions
200 g black lentils
600 ml vegetable stock
2 garlic cloves
50 g white cabbage
30 cherry tomatoes
2 1/2 limes
20 g ginger
curry powder
1 handful of coriander
1 handful of thyme
1 handful of parsley
1 handful of mint
100 g coconut pulp or coconut
flakes

For serving:
4 Tbsp. sour cream

APPLE-MANGO-RISOTTO

1 1/2 apples
1 ripe mango
80 g risotto rice
300 ml coconut milk
200 ml water
120 g cane sugar
1 orange
2 lemons
2 Tbsp. honey
3 Tbsp. coconut flakes
vegetable oil

STARTER

AROMATIC PEANUT SALAD

Ⓥ

MAIN DISH

BLACK LENTIL STEW

Ⓥ

DESSERT

APPLE-MANGO-RISOTTO

AROMATISCHER ERDNUSSSALAT
AROMATIC PEANUT SALAD

SALAT
Die Erdnüsse ohne Öl
in einer Pfanne langsam
anrösten. — Die rote
und grüne Paprika in feine
Würfel schneiden und
die gelbe in Streifen. —
Die Aubergine schälen,
in Würfel schneiden
und etwas salzen. Dann
in Kartoffelstärke wälzen,
in heißem Pflanzenöl
frittieren und zur Seite
stellen. — Die 4 Limetten
auspressen und den
Saft auffangen. Die Chili
und die Schalotten in sehr
feine Würfel schneiden
und kurz anbraten, mit Limettensaft ablöschen.
Den Ingwer schälen und fein
dazu reiben. Den Korian-
der fein hacken und die
Mango in Würfel schneiden.

ZUM ANRICHTEN
Alle vorbereiteten Zutaten in
eine Schüssel geben. — Mit
Salz, Rohrzucker und etwas
Sesamöl abschmecken.

SALAD
Slowly dryroast the peanuts
in a pan. — Cut the red
and green pepper into cubes
and the yellow pepper
into strips. — Peel the eggplant and season with
salt. Then roll the eggplant
in corn starch, deep-fry
in hot oil until golden and
set aside. — Juice the
lime and set aside. Finely
chop the chili and shal-
lots and fry briefly, deglaze
with lime juice. Peel the
ginger, finely grate and cook
together with the chili
and shallots. — Finely chop
the coriander and cube
the mango.

FOR SERVING
In a bowl mix the coriander
and mango with all the
other prepared ingredients.
— Season with salt, a
pinch of cane sugar and a
splash of sesame oil.

BUNTER EINTOPF MIT SCHWARZEN LINSEN
BLACK LENTIL STEW

EINTOPF

Das Gemüse waschen, schälen und in mundgerechte Stücke schneiden und die Zwiebeln fein würfeln. — Etwas Pflanzenöl in einem Topf erhitzen, die Zwiebeln hinzugeben und anbraten. Im Anschluss die schwarzen Linsen hinzufügen, anbraten und mit Gemüsefond ablöschen. — Dann den Sellerie, die Süßkartoffel und die Karotten hinzugeben und mitköcheln lassen. — Den Knoblauch sehr fein hacken und dazugeben. Abdecken und 10 Minuten köcheln lassen. — Ingwer in grobe Scheiben schneiden und mitkochen. — Das Weißkraut in feine Streifen schneiden und die Tomaten würfeln. Beides mit Salz und Zucker abschmecken und in einer Schüssel mit Limettensaft marinieren. 5 Minuten ziehen lassen und im An-

schluss mit in den Eintopf geben und für weitere 15 Minuten köcheln lassen. — Das Gemüse im Topf mit etwas Curry abschmecken und sobald die Linsen gar sind, mit Salz würzen. — Die Kräuter fein hacken und dazugeben. Das Kokosnussfleisch in Streifen schneiden, dazugeben und 1–2 Minuten mitkochen.

ZUM ANRICHTEN

Den bunten Eintopf in einer Schüssel servieren und mit Sauerrahm verfeinern.

Tipp: Alternativ zum Kokosnussfleisch können auch 100 g Kokosflocken verwendet werden. Zuvor für 30 Minuten in Wasser einweichen und diese als Ersatz benutzen.

LENTIL STEW

Peel the vegetables and cut them into bite-sized pieces. Finely chop the onion. — Put some vegetable oil in a saucepan and fry the onion. Then add the lentils, fry and deglaze them with the vegetable stock. — Add celery, sweet potato and carrots and cook together with the rest. — Finely chop the garlic and add to the other vegetables. Cover and let it simmer for 10 minutes. — Slice the ginger and add to the vegetables. — Cut the white cabbage into strips, cube tomatoes, place them together in a bowl, add lime juice and allow to sit for 5 minutes. — Then add to the stew and let simmer for another 15 minutes. — Season the vegetables in the saucepan with a pinch of curry powder and once the lentils are done, season

with salt. — Chop the herbs finely and add to the cooked vegetables. Cut the coconut pulp into strips, add to the vegetables and cook for 1–2 minutes.

FOR SERVING

Serve the stew in a bowl and refine with sour cream.

Tip: As an alternative to the coconut pulp, 100 g coconut flakes can be used. Allow to soak in water for 30 minutes beforehand and use this as a replacement.

APFEL-MANGO-RISOTTO
APPLE-MANGO-RISOTTO

RISOTTO

Die Kokosmilch mit 200 ml Wasser, Zucker und Honig in einem Topf verrühren und kurz aufkochen lassen. — Die Äpfel in feine Würfel schneiden und im Anschluss in einem Topf mit etwas Pflanzenöl kurz andünsten und danach den Reis hinzugeben. Nun Schritt für Schritt die Kokosmilch zum Reis hinzugeben: mit je 5 Minuten Abstand je eine Kelle der Kokosmilch zum Reis geben und so langsam garen. — Die Schale der Zitronen und der Orange abreiben und die Früchte entsaften. Die Mango schälen und in einem Mixer pürieren, den Orangen- und Zitronensaft hinzugeben und je 1 TL Zeste der Zitrusfrüchte unterrühren. — Das Mangopüree unter das Risotto rühren. — Zum Schluss das Risotto mit Kokosflocken garnieren.

RISOTTO

Mix the coconut milk with 200 ml of water, sugar and honey in a saucepan and bring to the boil. Set aside. — Cut the apples into small cubes and sauté briefly in a pan with some vegetable oil, then add the rice. Now gradually add the coconut milk to the rice: every 5 minutes add one ladleful of coconut milk to the rice in order to slowly cook through. — Grate the orange and lemon peel and juice the fruits. Peel mango and puree in a blender. Then add the orange and lemon juice to the coconut rice, and 1 tsp. of each, grated lemon and orange peel. — Stir in the mango puree. Garnish with coconut flakes.

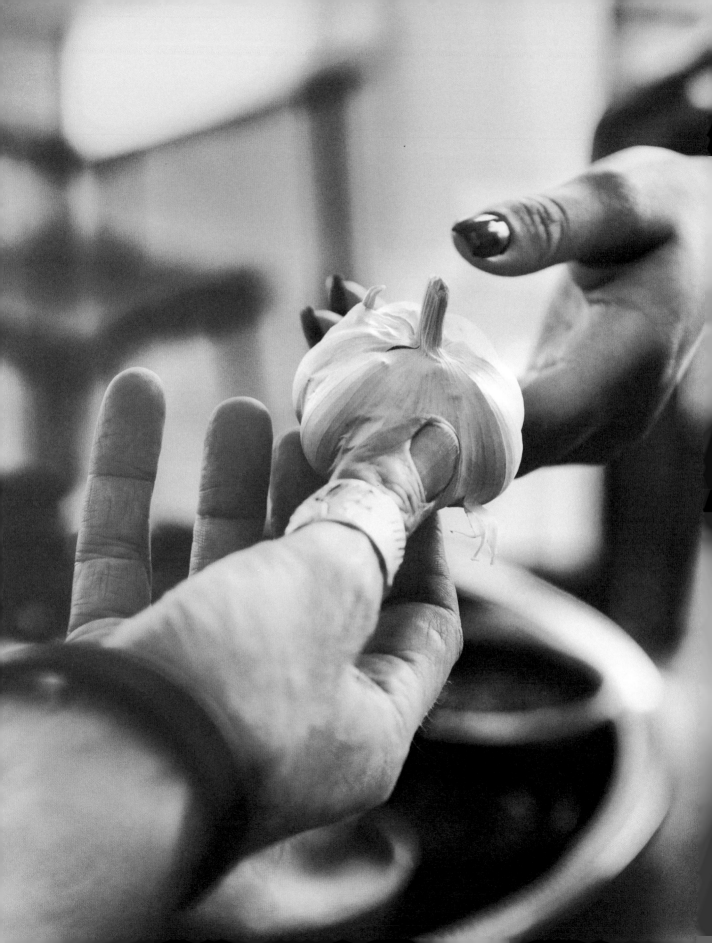

4

ROSINEN, CASHEWS, KARDAMOM: DAS GEDÄCHTNIS STÄRKEN

RAISINS, CASHEWS, CARDAMOM: ENHANCING YOUR MEMORY

ALAA & RALF

Der Geschmack der syrischen Küche ist von Zitrone und Knoblauch geprägt und so durchziehen diese Düfte auch die Räume des Kitchen Hub, in denen Alaa und Ralf zusammen kochen. Es wird heute als Vorspeise das typisch syrische Familiengericht Foul geben, ein Bohnengericht, das gerne am Freitagmorgen, zu Beginn des Wochenendes im Kreis der vollzählig versammelten Familie gegessen wird. Dazu reicht Ralf einen frischen Gurkensalat – a perfect match! Als Hauptspeise wird ein Hühnchengericht zubereitet, als Nachspeise Grieß und Filoteig mit Beeren. Ralf kommt aus einer Gasthaus-Dynastie und ein gemeinsames Essen im Kreis der Familie ist meist nur einmal im Jahr, nämlich an Heiligabend, möglich.

Beide, Alaa und Ralf, sind sich einig, dass Essen mehr ist als Genuss, es wirkt auch ein auf unseren Körper und Geist. Rosinen und Cashews stärken das Gedächtnis, so gab es Alaas Großmutter weiter und Ralf schreibt dem Kardamom eine ähnliche Wirkung zu. Und falls wir uns mal überessen sollten bei all diesen wundervollen Gerichten: warmes Wasser mit Kreuzkümmel hilft zuverlässig. Achtung: Magie-Alarm!

Syrian cuisine is characterized by the tastes of lemon and garlic, whose scents fill the air of the Kitchen Hub, where Alaa and Ralf are cooking together. The typical Syrian family dish foul will be served as a starter today: a bean dish you usually have with the whole family gathered together on a Friday morning at the beginning of the weekend. Accompanying it, Ralf serves a fresh cucumber salad – a perfect match! A chicken dish is prepared for the main course, and semolina is on for dessert. Ralf comes from a family dynasty of restaurateurs. Sharing a meal with the family is usually, if at all, only possible once a year on Christmas Eve.

However, Alaa and Ralf both agree that eating is more than just pleasure; it affects the well-being of our body and soul. While Alaa's grandmother passed on the wisdom that raisins and cashews enhance your memory, Ralf ascribes a similar effect to cardamom. And if you should ever overeat yourself on all these wonderful dishes: warm water and cumin will help for sure. But attention: beware of magic!

58

MENÜ

VORSPEISE

FOUL MIT SESAM-FAVABOHNEN AN GURKENSALAT

HAUPTSPEISE

KNUSPRIGE HÄHNCHENSCHENKEL AN MANGOLD

NACHSPEISE

NUSSIGER FILOTEIG AN LIBANESISCHER NACHT MIT BEEREN

FOUL MIT SESAM-FAVABOHNEN AN GURKENSALAT

Für die Bohnen:
200 g Favabohnen
(dicke Bohnen)
100 g Tahini
80 g Joghurt
2 Knoblauchzehen
1 TL Kreuzkümmel
1 Zitrone
Salz

Für den Gurkensalat:
2 Salatgurken
1 rote Zwiebel
15 – 20 g frischer Dill
1 Prise Zucker
1 Zitrone
80 ml Essig (8 EL)
4 EL Pflanzenöl
2 TL Koriandersamen
Salz

Zum Anrichten:
50 g Wildreis
Salz
Sumak
Kreuzkümmel
frische Granatapfelkerne

KNUSPRIGE HÄHNCHENSCHENKEL AN MANGOLD

Für die Hähnchenschenkel:
4 Hähnchenschenkel
2 Knoblauchzehen
1 TL Kreuzkümmel
1 Orange
1 Prise Zimt
4 Kardamomkapseln,
gemörsert
2 Thymianzweige
1 kleiner Rosmarinzweig

Für den Mangold:
800 g Mangold
2 1/2 EL Ghee
oder Butterschmalz
3 Knoblauchzehen
1 EL Koriandersamen
120 ml Hühnerfond
3 Schalotten
Salz
Pfeffer

Für den Reis:
100 g Fadennudeln
250 g Basmatireis
ca. 500 ml Wasser
1 Lorbeerblatt

NUSSIGER FILOTEIG AN LIBANESISCHER NACHT MIT BEEREN

Für die libanesische Grießspeise:
200 ml Wasser
200 g Zucker
500 ml Milch
150 g Hartweizengrieß
1 EL Zucker
1 EL Rosenwasser
200 g Crème Double
3 EL Puderzucker

Für den nussigen Filoteig:
350 g blanchierte Mandeln
30 g Puderzucker
2 TL Zimt
8 Blätter küchenfertiger
Filoteig
110 g Butter

Zum Anrichten:
200 g frische Beeren

SESAME-BROAD BEANS FOUL AND CUCUMBER SALAD

For the beans:
200 g broad beans
100 g tahini
80 g yoghurt
2 garlic cloves
1 tsp. cumin
1 lemon
salt

For the cucumber salad:
2 cucumbers
1 red onion
15 – 20 g dill
1 pinch of sugar
1 lemon
80 ml white vinegar (8 Tbsp.)
4 Tbsp. vegetable oil
2 tsp. coriander seeds
salt

For serving:
50 g wild rice
salt
sumac
cumin
fresh pomegranate seeds

CRISPY CHICKEN WINGS WITH CHARD

For the chicken wings:
4 chicken wings
2 garlic cloves
1 tsp. cumin
1 orange
1 pinch of cinnamon
4 cardamom capsules, ground
2 thyme sprigs
1 rosemary sprig

For the chard:
800 g chard
2 1/2 Tbsp. ghee
or clarified butter
3 garlic cloves
1 Tbsp. coriander seeds
120 ml chicken stock
3 shallots
salt
pepper

For the rice:
100 g vermicelli
250 g basmati rice
approx. 500 ml water
1 bay leaf

NUTTY PHYLLO PASTRY AT LIBANESE NIGHT WITH BERRIES

For the semolina porridge:
200 ml water
200 g sugar
500 ml water
150 g semolina
1 Tbsp. sugar
1 Tbsp. rosewater
200 g heavy cream
3 Tbsp. powdered sugar

For the phyllo pastry:
350 g blanched almonds
30 g powdered sugar
2 tsp. cinnamon
8 sheets ready
to cook phyllo pastry
110 g butter

For serving:
200 g seasonal berries

MENUE
SERVES 4

STARTER

SESAME-BROAD BEANS FOUL AND CUCUMBER SALAD

MAIN DISH

CRISPY CHICKEN WINGS WITH CHARD

DESSERT

NUTTY PHYLLO PASTRY AT LIBANESE NIGHT WITH BERRIES

FOUL MIT SESAM-FAVABOHNEN AN GURKENSALAT
SESAME-BROAD BEANS FOUL AND CUCUMBER SALAD

BOHNEN

Die Bohnen über Nacht einweichen und dann gar kochen. — Die Zitrone auspressen und den Saft mit Joghurt, Tahina und Kreuzkümmel mischen. Den geschälten Knoblauch sehr fein hacken und zu der Mischung geben. Die Joghurt-Tahina-Mischung zu den Bohnen geben und kurz erwärmen. Mit Salz abschmecken.

GURKENSALAT

Die Gurken schälen, das Kerngehäuse entfernen und die Gurken in dünne Scheiben schneiden. Eine Prise Salz und eine Prise Zucker dazugeben. Den Dill fein hacken, die Schale der Zitrone abreiben und die Frucht entsaften. — Die rote Zwiebel in feine Ringe schneiden und in ca. 6 EL Weißweinessig einlegen. — Die Koriandersamen ohne Öl leicht rösten und danach in einem Mörser zermahlen. Dann die Gurken mit 4 EL Pflanzenöl, 2 EL Weißweinessig, 1–2 EL Zitronensaft, Zitronenzeste, gemahlenen Koriandersamen und Dill abschmecken und mit den eingelegten Zwiebeln garnieren.

ZUM ANRICHTEN

Den Wildreis in sehr heißem Öl frittieren, bis er aufgepufft ist. Das Öl durch ein Sieb abgießen und den gepufften Wildreis auf Küchenpapier entfetten. Mit Salz, Kreuzkümmel und etwas Sumak würzen, über den Gurkensalat geben und zusammen mit dem Foul servieren. Mit frischen Granatapfelkernen dekorieren.

BEANS

Allow the beans to soak overnight and then cook them until soft. — Juice the lemon and mix the juice with yoghurt, tahini and cumin. Finely chop the garlic and add it to the mixture. Pour the yoghurt-tahini mix over the cooked beans, heat up again and season with salt.

CUCUMBER SALAD

Peel the cucumber, remove the seeds and cut into thin slices. Mix with a pinch of salt and sugar. Finely chop the dill, finely grate the lemon peel and juice the fruit. — Cut the red onion into thin slices, place into 6 Tbsp. white vinegar and let sit. — Slightly toast the coriander seeds in a pan without using oil and grind the roasted seeds in a mortar. Then season the cucumber salad with 4 Tbsp. vegetable oil, 2 Tbsp. white vinegar, 1–2 Tbsp. lemon juice, grated lemon peel, ground coriander seeds and dill. Garnish with pickled onions.

FOR SERVING

Deep-fry wild rice in very hot oil until it is puffed. Drain puffed wild rice through a sieve and degrease it on paper towels. Season with salt, cumin and sumac, add to the cucumber salad and serve together with the foul. Garnish with fresh pomegranate seeds.

KNUSPRIGE HÄHNCHENSCHENKEL AN MANGOLD
CRISPY CHICKEN WINGS WITH CHARD

HÄHNCHENSCHENKEL

Die Kräuter und den Knoblauch fein hacken und die Schale der Orange abreiben. — Den Röhrenknochen von dem Hähnchenschenkel lösen. Den Schenkel mit der Hautseite nach unten zeigend flach auf ein Brett drücken. Die Kräuter mit dem Knoblauch, der Orangenzeste, dem Kardamom, Zimt und dem Kreuzkümmel vermengen und damit die Innenseite des Hähnchenschenkels einreiben. Anschließend auf der Hautseite für ca. 5 Minuten bei mittlerer Stufe anbraten und danach im Ofen bei 170°C für ca. 25 Minuten auf der Hautseite garen.

MANGOLD

Mangold keilförmig vom Stiel abtrennen und in mundgerechte Stücke schneiden. Den Knoblauch und die Schalotten fein würfeln. — Etwas Öl in eine Pfanne geben und die Koriandersamen sowie den Knoblauch kurz darin andünsten, bis die Samen und der Knoblauch goldbraun sind. Danach zur Seite stellen. — Ghee in einer extra Pfanne schmelzen lassen und die gewürfelten Schalotten dazugeben. Anschließend den Mangold hinzugeben und kurz andünsten. Mit dem Hühnerfond ablöschen und einige Minuten kochen lassen, bis der Mangold weich ist. Die gerösteten Koriandersamen und Knoblauch hinzugeben und mit Salz und Pfeffer würzen.

REIS

Die Nudeln kurz in heißem Öl anbraten, den Reis hinzugeben, kurz mitdünsten und dann mit ca. 500 ml Wasser aufgießen. Etwas Salz und ein Lorbeerblatt hinzugeben und für ca. 20 Minuten garen lassen. — Nun den Reis zusammen mit dem pikanten Mangold und den knusprigen Hähnchenschenkeln servieren.

CHICKEN WINGS

Finely chop the herbs and grate the orange peel. Remove the long bone of the chicken wing. Flatten the wings with the skinny side facing downwards on a cutting board. Mix the herbs with garlic, grated orange peel, cardamom, cinnamon and cumin, and rub on the inside of the chicken wings. Then fry the chicken wings' skinny side downwards over medium heat for 5 minutes. Put the skinny side downwards in the oven at 170°C for 25 minutes in order to cook through.

CHARD

Remove bottom ends of the chard and cut into small pieces. Finely cube garlic cloves and shallots. Heat some oil in a pan and briefly fry coriander seeds and garlic until they are golden brown. Set aside. — Melt ghee in another pan and fry the cubed shallots, then add chard and briefly sauté together. Pour in the chicken stock and cook for a few minutes until the chard is tender. Add roasted coriander seeds and garlic, and season with salt and pepper.

RICE

Briefly fry vermicelli in hot oil, add the rice and briefly sauté, then add the water. Cook rice with a pinch of salt and one bay leaf for 20 minutes or until cooked through. — Now serve the rice together with the savory chard and the crunchy chicken legs.

NUSSIGER FILOTEIG AN LIBANESISCHER NACHT MIT BEEREN
NUTTY PHYLLO PASTRY AT LIBANESE NIGHT WITH BERRIES

GRIESSSPEISE

Zuerst in einem kleinen Kochtopf 200 g Zucker mit 200 ml Wasser zum Kochen bringen und ca. 6 Minuten köcheln lassen, bis ein Sirup entsteht. Vom Herd nehmen und auskühlen lassen. — In einem großen Kochtopf die Milch mit dem Grieß, 1 EL Zucker und dem Rosenwasser vermischen. Bei hoher Hitze unter ständigem Rühren zum Kochen bringen und 3 – 4 Minuten lang köcheln lassen, bis die Masse eingedickt ist. Den Grießbrei in eine großflächige Schüssel geben und auskühlen lassen. — Die Crème Double mit dem Puderzucker vermengen und auf dem abgekühlten Grießbrei verteilen. — Vor dem Servieren den Sirup löffelweise darüber geben.

FILOTEIG

Den Backofen auf 180°C vorheizen. Mandeln grob hacken und in einer Schüssel mit dem Puderzucker und Zimt vermengen, beiseitestellen. — Die Filoteigblätter auf einer Arbeitsfläche übereinander stapeln. Mit einem scharfen Messer und einem 10 cm großen Unterteller als Schablone insgesamt 8 Kreise aus dem Teigstapel schneiden. — Backpapier auf einem Backblech auslegen und währenddessen die Butter langsam zerlassen. Darauf zwei Teigkreise übereinanderlegen, jeweils eingepinselt mit zerlassener Butter und das obere Blatt mit einem gestrichenen Esslöffel der Mandelmischung bestreuen. — Für 20 – 25 Minuten auf mittlerer Schiene goldbraun backen.

ZUM ANRICHTEN

Die frischen Beeren waschen und gemeinsam mit dem nussigen Filoteig und der libanesischen Grießspeise servieren.

SEMOLINA PORRIDGE

Slowly boil 200 ml water and 200 g sugar for 6 minutes until a syrup has formed. Take off the stove in order to cool down. — In a big pot, mix milk with semolina, 1 Tbsp. of sugar and the rosewater. Bring to the boil on high heat and cook for 3 – 4 minutes, stirring constantly until the mass starts to thicken. Pour semolina porridge in a big bowl and allow to cool down. — Mix the heavy cream with the powdered sugar and pour over the cooled semolina porridge. Before serving, drizzle the syrup on top of it using a tablespoon.

PHYLLO DOUGH

Preheat oven to 180°C. Coarsely chop almonds and mix together with powdered sugar and cinnamon, set aside. — Place the phyllo pastry on a work surface. Using a 10 cm-wide plate as a template and a sharp knife, cut 8 circles from the phyllo pastry. — Line baking paper in a baking tray and melt butter slowly. Then place two phyllo pastry circles each brushed with melted butter on the baking paper and sprinkle the top circle with one tablespoon of the almond-powdered sugar mix. Bake in the preheated oven for 20 – 25 minutes until golden.

FOR SERVING

Wash the berries and serve together with the nutty phyllo dough and the Lebanese semolina porridge.

5

TSCHAPATI GEHT IMMER
CHAPATI? ALWAYS

WAJID & SEBASTIAN

Wenn ein deutsches Bauernfrühstück gereicht wird, dann schmeckt es auch Wajid besonders gut. Obwohl das Brot fehlt und das ist in Pakistan eher selten. Das pakistanische Brot Tschapati stellt dort nicht nur zum Frühstück ein Grundnahrungsmittel dar. Die brotliebenden Pakistaner ähneln also doch sehr den Deutschen mit ihrer Vorliebe für verschiedenste Brotsorten. In der Küche des Restaurants Horváth wird also nicht nur gekocht, sondern auch gebacken, und zwar gemeinsam von Wajid aus Pakistan und Sebastian aus Niederösterreich. An den Heimatküchen der beiden Köche zeigt sich die Fusionsdimension auch der traditionellen Küchen: Sebastian erzählt von der Küche seiner niederösterreichischen Heimat, die durch verschiedene Kochtraditionen aus Ungarn, Böhmen und Norditalien beeinflusst wurde. Auch Pakistans kulinarische Traditionen hängen eng mit denen seiner Nachbarn, vor allem Indien, zusammen. Es wird scharf gegessen, viel Reis, viel Fleisch, stets warme Mahlzeiten, stets selbstgekocht und Gastfreundlichkeit steht dabei immer an erster Stelle. Als Sebastian sein Interesse an einer genaueren Erkundung der pakistanischen Küche zu erkennen gibt, lässt Wajids herzliche Einladung zu sich nach Hause nicht lange auf sich warten. Schließlich wurden wir ebenso herzlich im Restaurant in Empfang genommen. Eine glückliche Fusionsbegegnung wie diese beruht immer auf Gegenseitigkeit. Darauf stoßen wir mit einem aromatischen pakistanischen Chai mit grünem Kardamom an!

Whenever a German farmer's breakfast is served, Wajid is delighted. Although it is served without bread, which is definitely the exception in Pakistani cuisine. The Pakistani bread Chapati is not only a basic ingredient for breakfast. Rather, the bread-loving Pakistanis much more resemble the Germans in their love for all different kinds of bread. In the kitchen of the Restaurant Horváth the two chefs Wajid from Pakistan and Sebastian from Lower Austria are thus not just cooking, but baking together as well. From their native countries' cuisines you can tell that a fusion-dimension is already a part of many traditional cuisines: Sebastian tells us about the Lower Austrian cuisine, which is influenced by diverse cooking traditions from Hungary, Bohemia and Northern Italy. Pakistan's culinary practices, too, are closely linked to their neighbors', especially India. Meals are spicy, made with a lot of rice, a lot of meat, always warm, always home-cooked, and the doors are always open for everyone to join. Thus, as Sebastian seems to have taken a great interest in discovering more of Pakistani cuisine, it is not long before Wajid cordially invites him to his home. After all, the welcome we received to his restaurant today was just as warm. Happy fusion-encounters like this one are always based on reciprocity, which is also what we toast to today with an aromatic Pakistani chai with green cardamom!

MENÜ

FÜR 4 PERSONEN

VORSPEISE

DEUTSCH-PAKISTANISCHE DIP-VARIATIONEN MIT BROT & SALAT

HAUPTSPEISEN

KICHERERBSEN-DHAL

GEFÜLLTE PAPRIKA MIT PARADEISKRAUT

NACHSPEISE

KARAMELLISIERTE KAROTTEN-GRIESSNOCKEN-FUSION

WAJID & SEBASTIAN

DEUTSCH-PAKISTANI-SCHE DIP-VARIATIONEN MIT BROT & SALAT

Für den Brotteig:
200 g Weizenmehl
200 g Vollkornmehl
ca. 200 ml lauwarmes Wasser
1 *Prise* Salz
Pflanzenöl zum Anbraten
ca. 50 g Butter

Für die Marillenkerncreme:
150 g süße Marillenkerne
(ersatzweise Mandeln)
100 ml Milch
Salz
1 Zitrone
2 EL Marillenkernöl

Für den Walnuss-Dip:
1 grüne Chili
100 g Walnüsse
50 g geschälte Mandeln
1 1/2 EL getrocknete
Granatapfelkerne
6 Kirschtomaten
4 EL Pflanzenöl
6 EL Wasser
1 EL Naturjoghurt
Salz

Für den Chili-Dip:
2 grüne Chilis
4 Kirschtomaten
30 Minzblätter
1 Zwiebel
4 EL Wasser
1 EL Naturjoghurt
Salz

Für den Waldmeisteressig:
100 g frischer Waldmeister
600 ml Wasser
400 g Zucker
50 ml Gemüsefond
50 ml Weißweinessig
50 ml naturtrüber Apfelsaft

Zum Anrichten:
200 g Blattsalat

KICHERERBSEN-DHAL

350 g Kichererbsen
1 EL Ghee oder
Butterschmalz
1 EL Tomatenmark
100 ml Gemüsefond
1 *große* Zwiebel
6 Knoblauchzehen
20 g Ingwer
3 *große* Tomaten
2 grüne Chilis
1 EL Kreuzkümmelsamen
1 TL Chilipulver
1/2 TL Kurkumapulver
1 TL gemahlener Koriander
Salz
1 Zitrone
1 *Handvoll* frischer Koriander

GEFÜLLTE PAPRIKA MIT PARADEISKRAUT

Für die gefüllte Paprika:
4 rote Spitzpaprika
150 g Kichererbsen
50 ml Gemüsefond
1 Knoblauchzehe
2 Schalotten
3 EL Crème fraîche
1 *Handvoll* frische Petersilie
2 *Msp.* Zitronenabrieb
1 *Msp.* gemahlener Kümmel
Salz, Pfeffer, Muskat
Pflanzenöl

Für das Paradeiskraut:
200 g Weißkohl
1 Knoblauchzehe
1 Zwiebel
1 EL Tomatenmark
1 *Schuss* Weißwein
1 EL Zucker
1 Lorbeerblatt
6 Tomaten
Pflanzenöl
Salz, Pfeffer

Zum Anrichten:
100 g Sauerrahm

KARAMELLISIERTE KAROTTEN-GRIESS-NOCKEN-FUSION

*Für die
karamellisierten
Karotten:*
20 Bleistiftmöhren
1 EL Butter
1 EL Zucker

Für die Kürbiskernöl-Nocken:
100 ml Milch
50 g weiße Schokolade
100 ml Kürbiskernöl
50 g Weizengrieß

Für das Karotten-Halwa:
250 g Karotten
1 EL Ghee
1 EL Weizengrieß
1 EL geraspelte Mandeln
250 ml Milch
2 EL Zucker
1 1/2 EL Rosinen
2 Kardamomkapseln

Zum Anrichten:
100 g Kürbiskerne
5 EL Kürbiskernöl
Salz
5 EL Vanillezucker
mit echter Vanille

SPICY DIP VARIATION WITH PAN BREAD AND FRESH SALAD

For the dough:
200 g wheat flour
200 g wholemeal flour
approx. 200 ml water, lukewarm
1 pinch of salt
vegetable oil for frying
50 g butter

For the apricot kernel cream:
150 g sweet apricot kernels (or almonds)
100 ml milk
salt
1 lemon
2 Tbsp. apricot kernel oil

For the walnut dip:
1 green chili
100 g walnuts
50 g peeled almonds
1 1/2 Tbsp. dried pomegranate seeds
6 cherry tomatoes
4 Tbsp. vegetable oil
6 Tbsp. water
1 Tbsp. plain yoghurt
salt

For the chili dip:
2 green chilis
4 cherry tomatoes
30 mint leaves
1 onion
4 Tbsp. water
1 Tbsp. plain yoghurt
salt

For the woodruff vinegar:
100 g fresh woodruff
600 ml water
400 g sugar
50 ml vegetable stock
50 ml white vinegar
50 ml apple juice

For serving:
200 g fresh salad

CHICKPEA DHAL

350 g chickpeas
1 Tbsp. ghee or clarified butter
1 Tbsp. tomato paste
100 ml vegetable stock
1 large onion
6 garlic cloves
20 g ginger
3 big tomatoes
2 green chilis
1 Tbsp. cumin seeds
1 Tbsp. chili powder
1/2 tsp. turmeric powder
1 tsp. coriander
salt
1 lemon

STUFFED PEPPERS WITH PARADEIS CABBAGE

For the stuffed peppers:
4 red pointed peppers
150 g soaked chickpeas
50 ml vegetable stock
1 garlic clove
2 shallots
3 Tbsp. crème fraîche
1 handful fresh parsley
2 pinches grated lemon peel
1 pinch cumin
salt
pepper
nutmeg
vegetable oil

For the Paradeis cabbage:
200 g white cabbage
1 garlic clove
1 onion
1 Tbsp. tomato paste
1 dash of white wine
1 Tbsp. sugar
1 bay leaf
6 tomatoes
vegetable oil
salt, pepper

For serving:
100 g sour cream

FUSION OF CARAMELIZED CARROTS AND SEMOLINA DUMPLINGS

For the caramelized carrots:
20 small carrots
1 Tbsp. butter
1 Tbsp. sugar

For the pumpkin seed oil dumplings:
100 ml milk
50 g white chocolate
100 ml pumpkin seed oil
50 g semolina

For the carrot halva:
250 g carrots
2 Tbsp. ghee or clarified butter
1 Tbsp. semolina
1 Tbsp. almonds
250 ml milk
2 Tbsp. sugar
1 1/2 Tbsp. raisins
2 cardamom pods

For serving:
100 g pumpkin seeds
5 Tbsp. pumpkin seed oil
salt
5 Tbsp. vanilla sugar with real vanilla

MENUE

SERVES 4

(V)

STARTER

SPICY DIP VARIATION WITH
PAN BREAD
AND FRESH SALAD

(V)

MAIN DISHES

CHICKPEA DHAL

(V)

STUFFED PEPPERS
WITH PARADEIS CABBAGE

(V)

DESSERT

FUSION OF CARAMELIZED
CARROTS AND
SEMOLINA DUMPLINGS

WAJID & SEBASTIAN

DEUTSCH-PAKISTANISCHE DIP-VARIATIONEN MIT BROT & SALAT
SPICY DIP VARIATION WITH PAN BREAD AND FRESH SALAD

MARILLENCREME
Die Marillenkerne 24 Stunden in der Milch einweichen. Die Zitrone auspressen und den Saft auffangen. — Sobald die Marillenkerne eingeweicht sind, die Haut von den Kernen ziehen und mit Milch, Zitronensaft, etwas Salz sowie dem Marillenkernöl zu einer feinen Paste pürieren.

WALNUSS-DIP
Alle Zutaten in einem Mixer pürieren, bis eine homogene Masse entsteht. — Mit Naturjoghurt verfeinern bzw. entschärfen.

CHILI-DIP
Alle Zutaten in einem Mixer pürieren, bis eine homogene Masse entsteht. — Mit Naturjoghurt verfeinern bzw. entschärfen.

BROT
Alle Zutaten zu einem Teig vermengen. Der Teig sollte nicht zu weich und auch nicht zu fest sein. — Den Teig mit einem Nudelholz kreisförmig ausrollen. Kleine Stückchen Butter (jeweils ca. 5 g) auf den Teig legen und diesen dann umfalten, 3–4 mal wiederholen, danach wieder zu einer Kugel formen und erneut ausrollen. — Öl in einer Pfanne erhitzen, den Brotteig darin ausbacken, bis beide Seiten goldbraun sind.

WALDMEISTERESSIG
Den Waldmeister offen auslegen und ca. 2–3 Tage welken lassen. Das Wasser mit dem Zucker zu einem Sirup aufkochen und abkühlen. Den Waldmeister für 48 Stunden im Sirup einlegen und dann abseihen. Gemüsefond, Weißweinessig und Apfelsaft miteinander vermengen und mit dem Waldmeistersirup abschmecken. Damit den frischen Blattsalat würzen.

APRICOT KERNEL CREAM
Soak the apricot kernels in milk for 24 hours. Juice the lemon. — Once the apricot kernels have been soaked, peel them and mix together with milk, lemon juice, a pinch of salt and the apricot kernel oil until smooth.

WALNUT AND CHILI DIP
Mix all ingredients together until smooth. Use plain yoghurt to season or to give it a smoother texture.

BREAD
Knead all ingredients into a dough. The dough should not be too stiff or too soft. — Roll out the dough using a rolling pin. — Spread small pieces of butter (approx. 5 g each) onto the dough and then fold over, repeat 3–4 times, then knead the dough together into the form of a ball and roll it out again. — Heat oil in a pan and fry the dough until golden brown on both sides.

WOODRUFF VINEGAR
Line woodruff in an open space and allow to wither for 2–3 days. Bring water and sugar to the boil and allow to cool down. Add the woodruff to the syrup and let it soak for 48 hours. Then strain through a sieve and set the woodruff syrup aside. — Mix together the vegetable stock, white vinegar and apple juice, season with woodruff syrup. Season the fresh salad with the woodruff vinegar.

KICHERERBSEN-DHAL
CHICKPEA DHAL

DHAL

Die Kichererbsen über Nacht in Wasser einweichen. Danach in einem Dampfkochtopf mit 1 TL Salz für ca. 10 Minuten kochen. — Währenddessen den Ingwer fein hobeln und die Zwiebel sowie den Knoblauch in Streifen schneiden. Die Zitronenschale abreiben und den den Saft auspressen. Den Koriander grob hacken. — Die Kreuzkümmelsamen in einer Pfanne ohne Zugabe von Öl oder Butter für 3 Minuten rösten. — Im Anschluss 1 gehäuften EL Ghee oder Butterschmalz hinzufügen und darin den gehobelten Ingwer, die in Streifen geschnittene Zwiebel und den in Streifen geschnittenen Knoblauch scharf anbraten. — Tomaten und Chili würfeln, hinzugeben und ebenfalls 3 Minuten scharf anbraten. Im Anschluss die restlichen Gewürze hinzugeben und für 10 Minuten köcheln lassen. Dann die Kichererbsen unter das Gemüse mischen, die Gemüsebrühe hinzugeben und für weitere 15 Minuten einkochen. Eventuell mit etwas Wasser strecken. Am Ende den Saft und die Schale der Zitrone hinzufügen und mit frischem Koriander servieren.

DHAL

Allow the chickpeas to soak overnight. Once fully soaked, cook with 1 tsp. salt for 10 minutes in a pressure cooker. — Meanwhile, finely grate the ginger and chop the onion and garlic into fine strips. Grate the lemon peel and juice the lemon. Coarsely chop the fresh coriander. — Roast the cumin seeds for 3 minutes without using any oil or butter in a pan. — Add 1 Tbsp. of ghee or clarified butter and fry grated ginger, garlic and onions. — Cube the tomatoes and chilis, add to the pan and fry for another 3 minutes. Add the remaining spices and let it simmer for 10 minutes. Mix in the chickpeas and the vegetable stock and let it cook for 15 minutes. — If necessary, add some water. — At the end, add the lemon juice and peel and serve with freshly chopped coriander.

GEFÜLLTE PAPRIKA MIT PARADEISKRAUT
STUFFED PEPPERS WITH PARADEIS CABBAGE

GEFÜLLTE PAPRIKA
Die Kichererbsen über Nacht in Wasser einweichen. — Die Paprika mit dem Bunsenbrenner von außen schwärzen. Die geschwärzte Schale abwaschen, von der Paprika den Strunk entfernen und entkernen. — Knoblauch und Schalotten fein würfeln, in Pflanzenöl anschwitzen, Kichererbsen hinzufügen, mit Gemüsefond ablöschen und für mindestens 10 Minuten köcheln lassen, bis die Flüssigkeit verkocht ist. — Den weichgekochten Kichererbsenmix zerdrücken, mit Crème fraîche mischen und mit gehackter Petersilie, Zitronenabrieb, Kümmel, Salz, Pfeffer, Muskat vermischen. — Die Spitzpaprika mit der Kichererbsenmasse füllen und in einer Pfanne von allen Seiten anbraten.

PARADEISKRAUT
Tomaten überbrühen, schälen und würfeln. Den Weißkohl in feine Streifen schneiden. Die Zwiebel und den Knoblauch fein würfeln und anschwitzen. Weißkohl, Zucker und Tomatenmark hinzufügen und kurz mit anschwitzen. Mit einem Schuss Weißwein ablöschen, Lorbeerblatt und gewürfelte Tomaten hinzufügen und ca. 30 Minuten einkochen lassen. Mit Salz und Pfeffer abschmecken.

ZUM ANRICHTEN
Die gefüllten Paprika und das Paradeiskraut auf einem Teller anrichten. Den Sauerrahm glatt rühren und darüber geben.

STUFFED PEPPERS
Allow the chickpeas to soak overnight. — Char the peppers from the outside with a Bunsen burner. Wash the blackened peel, remove the pepper stalk and seeds. — Cube garlic and shallots, fry with vegetable oil in a pan, add chickpeas and pour vegetable stock in the pan. Let it simmer for at least 10 minutes until the liquid has boiled away. — Mash the cooked chickpea mixture mix with crème fraîche and chopped parsley, grated lemon peel, cumin, salt, pepper and nutmeg. — Fill the pointed peppers with the chickpea mass and fry in a pan from all sides.

PARADEIS CABBAGE
Pour boiling water over the tomatoes, peel and cube. Cut the cabbage into fine strips. Finely cube and sauté the onion and garlic. Add white cabbage, sugar and tomato paste and sauté together. Deglaze with a dash of white wine and add the bay leaf and cubed tomatoes. Cook for about 30 minutes and season with salt and pepper.

FOR SERVING
Place stuffed peppers and Paradeis cabbage on a plate. Stir the sour cream until smooth and pour over the peppers and cabbage.

KARAMELLISIERTE KAROTTEN-GRIESSNOCKEN-FUSION
FUSION OF CARAMELIZED CARROTS AND SEMOLINA DUMPLINGS

KARAMELLISIERTE KAROTTEN
Karotten waschen, in Butter mit Schale und Grün ca. 10 Minuten sehr dunkel rösten. Mit Zucker karamellisieren.

KÜRBISKERNÖL-NOCKEN
Die Schokolade in der Milch auflösen, das Öl hinein- rühren und im Anschluss kühl stellen. Kleine Nocken abstechen. Den Grieß in einer Kaffeemühle fein mahlen und in einer Pfanne dunkel rösten. Die Nocken im Grieß wälzen.

KAROTTEN-HALWA
Karotten schälen und fein raspeln. 1 EL Ghee in einem Topf erhitzen und die Karottenraspeln dazugeben. Bei mittlerer Hitze ca. 3–4 Minuten anbraten. In der Zwischen- zeit den Weizengrieß und die geraspelten Mandeln in einer Pfanne ca. 5 Minuten rösten und anschließend vom Herd nehmen. — Die Rosinen waschen und trocken tupfen. In einem großen Topf Milch und

Zucker gemeinsam mit den Rosinen zum Kochen bringen. Die Karottenraspeln und die Grießmasse un- terrühren und bei mittlerer Flamme unter ständigem Rühren 15 Minuten köcheln lassen. Das Ganze sollte am Schluss eine cremige Kon- sistenz haben. Sollte das Halwa zu flüssig sein, kann man noch etwas Grieß hinzugeben. — Anschlie- ßend den Kardamom im Mörser fein reiben und unter- mischen. Eventuell mit weiterem Zucker ab- schmecken und alles gut verrühren. Aus der Masse eine Nocke formen und gemeinsam mit den karamellisierten Karot- ten und den Kürbiskern- öl-Nocken anrichten.

ZUM ANRICHTEN
Kürbiskerne in einer Pfanne rösten, hacken und mit Öl, Salz und Vanillezucker vermischen. Danach über das Halwa, die karamellisierten Ka- rotten und die Kürbiskern- öl-Nocken geben.

CARAMELIZED CARROTS
Wash carrots, roast them with peel and greens in a pan with butter until really dark. Caramelize with sugar.

PUMPKIN SEED OIL DUMPLINGS
Melt the chocolate into the milk and stir into the oil. Allow to cool down. Cut little dumplings out of the mass. Finely grind semolina in a coffee mill and roast in a pan until dark. Roll the little dump- lings in the roasted semolina.

CARROT HALVA
Peel the carrots and finely grate. Heat up 1 Tbsp. of ghee in a sauce pan and add the grated carrots. Cook over medium heat for 3–4 minutes, constantly stirring. — Heat the remai- ning ghee and roast the semolina and almonds for 5 minutes. Remove from heat. — Wash the raisins and pat dry. In a big sau- cepan bring the milk with

the sugar and raisins to the boil. Stir in the grated carrots and semolina mixture. Simmer over me- dium heat for about 15 minutes, stirring constant- ly. At the end everything should have a creamy con- sistency. If the halva is too liquid, add a little bit more semolina. — At the end stir in the carda- mom pods, if necessary use sugar to sweeten and mix well. Form one big dumpling out of the mass and serve together with the caramelized carrots and pumpkin seed oil dumplings.

FOR SERVING
Roast pumpkin seeds in a pan, chop and mix with oil, salt and vanilla sugar. Sprinkle over halva, caramelized carrots and pumpkin seed oil dumpling.

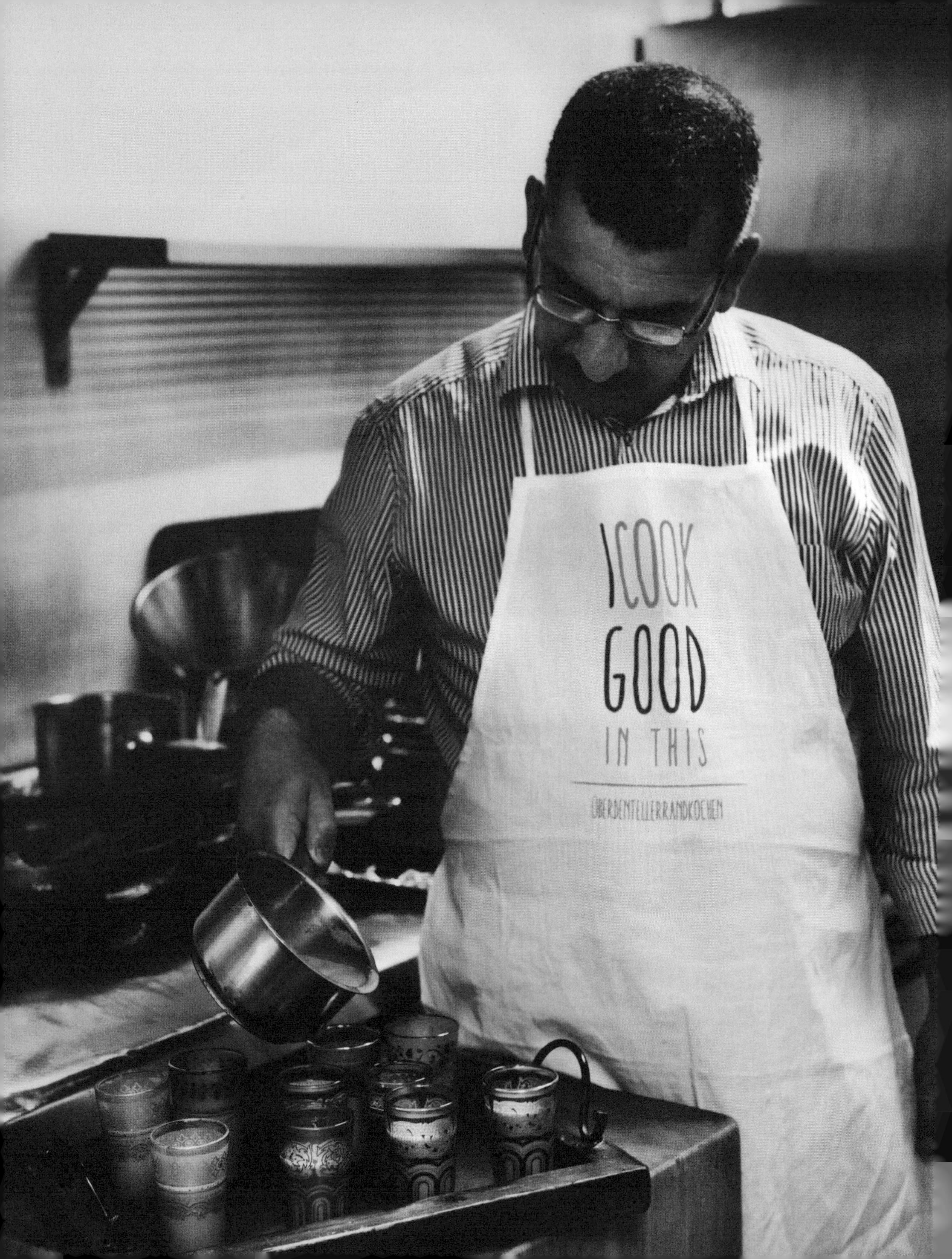
I COOK
GOOD
IN THIS
ÜBERDENTELLERRANDKOCHEN

CHAI TRADITIONEN
CHAI TRADITIONS

In Pakistan gehört Chai zum Alltag, in vielen Familien wird ein nicht unwesentlicher Teil des Haushaltseinkommens für Tee ausgegeben. Auch wenn grüner Tee ebenfalls sehr verbreitet ist, so ist es doch der schwarze Tee, serviert mit Milch, der die pakistanische Küche und ihre Gerichte typischerweise begleitet. Je nach Region werden diverse Varianten zubereitet, wie etwa der salzige, pinkfarbene Noon Chai mit Pistazien und Kardamom in Kaschmir oder der süße Doodh Pati in Karachi. Süß, salzig, aromatisch – die Chaikultur deckt ein breites Spektrum an Geschmäckern ab.

Der als traditionell verstandene Chai hat sich Mitte des 20. Jahrhunderts erfolgreich gegen die populärkulturelle „Invasion" des Kaffees behauptet. Inzwischen ist er wieder unumstrittenes Nationalgetränk, das in Straßenküchen und eleganten Teehäusern von allen Pakistanis genossen wird und so Gemeinschaft stiftet. Die Teebrauer werden Chai Wala genannt; ihre Teeküche, die durchaus auch mobil sein kann, nennen die Pakistanis Dhaba. In manchen Gegenden wird der Chai traditionell nur aus der Untertasse getrunken bzw. mit gespitzten Lippen geschlürft. Die Zubereitung findet, ähnlich wie in anderen asiatischen und eurasischen Teeküchen, mit dem Samowar statt. Zum Chai werden Süßigkeiten wie frittierte Teigbällchen (Gulab Jamun), gebackene Teigfäden (Jalebi) oder Halva mit Nusskrokant (Sohan Halwa) gereicht. Trotz des britisch-kolonialen Ursprungs des Chais ist er in seiner farbigen und aromatischen Vielfalt bis heute das Lieblingsgetränk Pakistans. Auf einen Chai eingeladen zu werden, das bedeutet eine Einladung zu Tee und Gespräch, gerne beide gleichermaßen anregend und damit ein ganz besonderer Genuss.

In Pakistan, chai is part of daily life, and in fact many families spend a considerable proportion of their household income on tea. Although green tea is common, it is black tea, served with milk, that typically accompanies Pakistani dishes. Even so, each region has its own distinct take on chai: in Kashmir, one will be served salty, pink-colored Noon Chai, while Karachi is home to sweet Doodh Pati. Sweet, salty, aromatic – the chai culture covers almost every variation of flavor!

In the middle of the 20th century, traditional chai successfully asserted itself against the "invasion" of coffee. Since then, it has reassumed its position as the undisputed national drink, which is served in street kitchens and teahouses alike, and which creates a sense of community between Pakistanis from all walks of life. The tea brewers are called Chai Wala; their tea kitchens, which they carry with them from place to place, are known as Dhaba. In some areas, chai is traditionally drunk from the saucer, or rather sipped with pursed lips. Like in other Asian and Eurasian tea cultures, chai is brewed in a samowar. With it, sweets like gulab jamun (fried milk dough balls), jalebi (sticky deep-fried wheat flour) or halva with nut pieces (sohan halva) are served. Despite its colonial British origin, chai, in all its colorful and aromatic varieties, is still by far the favorite Pakistani drink. Being invited for chai means coming together for tea and chatting – and both are pleasures one can't refuse!

6

MEZZE, FINGERFOOD, PETISCOS

MEZZE,
FINGERFOOD,
PETISCOS

SARA & SABINE

Für gemeinsames Party Snacking mit Freunden bieten sich inter-kontinentale Rezepte besonders an. Sabine und Sara nehmen ein gelungenes Fest voller Geselligkeit ins Visier und zaubern jede Menge fantastisch-kulinarische Variationen im Atelier Culinário: Hummus mit Roter Bete oder Kalamata Oliven, Hirse-Tabouleh mit Paranüssen, kleine Sfiha-Pizzen mit Lachstatar, Lamm, Spinat oder Guacamole sowie Limonade aus Damaskus mit Zitronengras.

Für Sara hat das Kochen und Essen in Deutschland eine große Bedeutung bekommen. Was selbstverständlich schien, ist jetzt ein Mittel gegen Heimweh und Sehnsucht sowie ein Weg geworden, in der neuen Heimat Fuß zu fassen. Sabine, Brasilianerin mit deutschen Wurzeln, hat schon früh von ihrer Großmutter, Bäcke-rin und Schauspielerin, die Kunst der Gastfreundschaft gelernt. Essen und Kochen verbindet und öffnet Herzen. Vor allem Frauen, so scheint es, haben das schon immer gewusst. Denn die Omas, Mütter und Schwestern sind in allen hier versammelten Geschichten die unbestrittenen Protagonistinnen.

Intercontinental recipes especially lend themselves to pre-pare snacks for a party with friends. Sabine and Sara have set their sights on a successful party with great company and will conjure up all sorts of fantastic culinary varia-tions in the Atelier Culinário: Hummus with red beet and Kalamata olives, millet-tabbouleh with Brazil nuts, small sfiha-pizzas with salmon tartar, lamb, spinach or guacamo-le as well as lemonade from Damascus with lemongrass.

For Sara, cooking and eating in Germany has taken a whole new meaning. What used to be a matter of course, has now become a means to cure homesickness, and a way to gain foothold in a new home country. Sabine, a Brazilian with German roots, already learned the art of hospitality early on from her grandmother, who was a baker and actress. Cooking and eating connects and opens hearts. As it appears, women have always known this - the grandmothers, aunts and sisters are the uncon-tested protagonists in all of the stories we have gathered here.

88

VARIATIONEN

FÜR 8 PERSONEN

—————

(v)

HUMMUS-DREIERLEI

(v)

HIRSE-PARANUSS-
TABOULEH

(v)

LABNEH MIT SALSA CRIOLLA
UND ARABISCHEM BROT

HERZHAFTE
SFIHA-VARIATIONEN

(v)

LIMONADE
MIT ZITRONENGRAS

HUMMUS-DREIERLEI

Für das Hummus-Grundrezept:
500 g getrocknete Kichererbsen
(alternativ 2 Dosen à 425 g)
1 EL Natron
3 Knoblauchzehen
160 g Tahina
100 ml Zitronensaft
180 ml eiskaltes Wasser
feines Meersalz
Cayennepfeffer
Olivenöl

Für den Rote Bete Hummus:
1/3 Hummus (ca. 400 g)
1 gekochte Rote Bete
1 EL Zitronensaft
geriebene Zitronenschale
einer halben Zitrone
1/2 TL Kreuzkümmel
1 1/2 EL Tahina
Olivenöl
Meersalz
Pfeffer aus der Mühle

Für den Kalamata Hummus:
1/3 Hummus (ca. 400 g)
120 g schwarze Kalamata
Oliven
2 TL Thymianblätter
1 EL Zitronensaft
1/2 Zitrone
Abrieb einer 1/2 Zitrone

HIRSE-PARANUSS-TABOULEH

200 g Hirse
500 ml Wasser
2 EL Pflanzenöl
200 g Paranüsse
(oder 240 g Mandeln)
6 Tomaten
12 Frühlingszwiebeln
600 g Petersilie
80 g frische Minze

80 ml Zitronensaft
feines Meersalz
Pfeffer aus der Mühle
200 ml Olivenöl
6 Mini Romanasalate

Zum Anrichten:
3 EL gehackte Nüsse zum
Bestreuen

LABNEH MIT SALSA CRIOLLA UND ARABISCHEM BROT

Für den Labneh:
1 kg griechischer oder
türkischer Joghurt, 10% Fett
1 Knoblauchzehe
1 TL Meersalz
50 ml Olivenöl

Für die Salsa Criolla:
1 Karotte
2 Schalotten
1 rote Paprika
1 rote Chilischote
1 EL frischer, gehackter
Koriander, davon nur
die Stiele und Wurzel
4 EL Limettensaft
3 EL Olivenöl
feines Meersalz
Pfeffer aus der Mühle
1 TL brauner Zucker

Für das arabische Brot:
1 Packung arabisches Brot
(6 Scheiben, 300 g)
5 EL Olivenöl
2 EL Sumak
1 1/2 TL Salz

HERZHAFTE SFIHA-VARIATIONEN (32 STÜCK)

Für den Teig:
1 kg Mehl
2 EL trockene Hefe
500 ml lauwarmes Wasser
oder Milch
2 TL Zucker
1 1/2 TL Salz
4 EL Olivenöl

Belag 1: Lammfleisch
1 Zwiebel
1 Handvoll Blattpetersilie
1 Tomate
200 g Lammhackfleisch
2 EL Zitronensaft
1 TL arabisches Siebengewürz
Cayennepfeffer
Meersalz
Schwarzer Pfeffer
Granatapfelkerne
zum Garnieren

Belag 2: Spinat und Feta
300 g Spinat (alternativ:
Endivienblätter oder Mangold)
2 EL Sonnenblumenöl
1 Knoblauchzehe
1/2 TL Cayenne Pfeffer
Meersalz
Pfeffer aus der Mühle
80 g Feta

Belag 3: Lachstartar
250 g frischer Lachs
3–4 Schalotten
1 Handvoll Blattpetersilie
1 Stange Staudensellerie
1/2 TL frischer, geraspelter
Ingwer
1 EL Olivenöl
Meersalz
Pfeffer aus der Mühle

Tabasco
Abrieb 1 Zitrone
1 EL Zitronensaft

Belag 4: Guacamole
1 Avocado, ca. 300 g
4 EL Zitronensaft
2 Schalotten
1 Chilischote
1 EL Korianderstiele
2 Tomaten
Meersalz
Pfeffer aus der Mühle

LIMONADE MIT ZITRONENGRAS

180 ml Zitronensaft
(6–7 Zitronen)
2 Handvoll frische
Minze (40 g)
1 Zitronengras
1 TL frischer Ingwer,
gewürfelt (15 g)
1 1/2 l Wasser
120 g Rohrzucker
Crushed Ice
Zitronenschnitze zur
Dekoration

HUMMUS TRIO

For the basic hummus:
500 g dried chickpeas
(alternatively *2 cans of 425 g*)
1 Tbsp. natron
3 garlic cloves
160 g tahini
100 ml lemon juice
180 ml ice cold water
fine sea salt
cayenne pepper
olive oil

For the red beet hummus:
1/3 hummus (*approx. 400 g*)
1 red beet, cooked (100 g)
1 Tbsp. Zitronensaft
zest of 1/2 lemon
1/2 tsp. cumin
1 1/2 Tbsp. tahini
olive oil
sea salt
pepper

For the Kalamata hummus:
1/3 hummus (*approx. 400 g*)
120 g black Kalamata olives
2 tsp. thyme leaves
1 Tbsp. lemon juice
zest of 1/2 lemon

MILLET BRAZIL NUT TABBOULEH

For the tabbouleh:
200 g millet
500 ml water
2 Tbsp. vegetable oil
200 g Brazil nuts
(or 240 g almonds)
6 tomatoes
12 spring onions
600 g parsley
80 g fresh mint
80 ml lemon juice (*8 Tbsp.*)
fine sea salt

pepper from the mill
200 ml olive oil
6 mini romaine lettuces heads

For serving:
3 Tbsp. nuts, chopped

LABNEH WITH SALSA CRIOLLA AND ARABIC BREAD

For the labneh:
1 kg yoghurt, 10% fat
1 garlic clove
1 tsp. sea salt
50 ml olive oil

For the salsa criolla:
1 carrot
2 shallots
1 red pepper
1 red chili
1 Tbsp. coriander stems and roots, chopped
4 Tbsp. lime juice
3 Tbsp. olive oil
fine sea salt
pepper form the mill
1 tsp. brown sugar

Arabic Bread:
1 package Arabic bread
(*6 slices, 300 g*)
5 Tbsp. olive oil
2 Tbsp. sumac
1 1/2 tsp. salt

SAVORY SFIHA-VARIATIONS

For the dough:
1 kg flour
2 Tbsp. dry yeast
500 ml water, lukewarm
2 tsp. sugar
1 1/2 tsp. salt
4 Tbsp. olive oil

Topping 1: minced lamb
1 onion
1 handful parsley
1 tomato
200 g minced lamb
2 Tbsp. lemon juice
1 tsp. Arabic 7-spice
cayenne pepper
sea salt
black pepper from the mill
pomegranate seeds and
parsley or chive for garnish

Topping 2: spinach and feta
300 g spinach (alternatively,
endive leaves or chard)
2 Tbsp. vegetable oil
1 garlic clove
1/2 tsp. cayenne peper
sea salt
pepper from the mill
80 g feta

Topping 3: salmon tartar
250 g fresh salmon
3–4 shallots
1 handful parsley
1 celery stalk
1/2 tsp. fresh ginger, grated
1 Tbsp. olive oil
sea salt
pepper from the mill
Tabasco
zest of 1 lemon
1 Tbsp. lemonjuice

Topping 4: guacamole
1 avocado, *approx. 300 g*
4 Tbsp. lemon juice
2 shallots
1 chili
1 Tbsp. coriander stems
2 tomatoes
sea salt
pepper from the mill

LEMONADE WITH LEMONGRASS

180 ml lemon juice
(6–7 lemons)
2 handful fresh mint
(40 g)
1 lemongrass
1 tsp. fresh ginger, diced
(15 g)
1 1/2 l water
120 g cane sugar
crushed ice
lemon wedges
for decoration

VARIATIONS

(v)

HUMMUS TRIO

(v)

MILLET BRAZIL NUT
TABBOULEH

(v)

LABNEH WITH SALSA
CRIOLLA AND
ARABIC BREAD

SAVORY
SFIHA-VARIATIONS

(v)

LEMONADE WITH
LEMONGRASS

HUMMUS-DREIERLEI
HUMMUS TRIO

(v)

HUMMUS

Die Kichererbsen ca. 8 Stunden in 1,5 l kaltem Wasser und Natron einweichen lassen. Danach unter kaltem Wasser abspülen, abtropfen lassen und in einen großen Topf mit reichlich Wasser geben. — Ca. 1 Stunde köcheln, bis sie sehr weich sind. In einem Sieb abtropfen lassen. — Geschälten Knoblauch mit Salz zu einer Paste zerstampfen. Tahina im Glas gut verrühren, damit sich eine homogene Masse bildet. — Zusammen mit den Kichererbsen, der Knoblauchpaste, dem Zitronensaft und eiskaltem Wasser cremig pürieren. — Mit Salz und Cayennepfeffer abschmecken. Den Hummus in 3 Portionen teilen.

ROTE BETE HUMMUS

Rote Bete schälen, in Würfel schneiden und zum Hummus geben. — Mit einem Pürierstab mixen bis eine sehr cremige Masse entsteht. — Mit etwas Zitronensaft, Zitronenschale, Kreuzkümmel, Tahina, Salz und Pfeffer abschmecken.

Tipp: Die rote Bete entfaltet ihre Farbe und ihren Geschmack stärker, wenn sie roh in Alufolie gewickelt im Ofen gebacken wird.

KALAMATA HUMMUS

Oliven entkernen und mit den Thymianblättern und dem Hummus vermengen. — Dann mit einem Pürierstab cremig mixen. Mit Zitronensaft und Zitronenschale abschmecken.

ZUM ANRICHTEN

Die drei fertigen Hummussorten auf Schüsselchen verteilen und mit Olivenöl und knusprigem, arabischen Brot servieren.

Tipp: Für eine grüne Variante, frische Kräuter pürieren, unter den Hummus mischen und kräftig abschmecken.

HUMMUS

Allow the chickpeas to soak 8 hours with 1.5 l cold water and 2 Tbsp. natron. Rinse the chickpeas under cold water and drain. — Put the chickpeas in a pot with plenty of water and let simmer for approx. 1 hour until soft. Drain the chickpeas again. — Grind the garlic with a pinch of salt in a mortar (or on a cutting board with a knife) and mash into a paste. Mix the chickpeas, tahini, garlic paste, lemon juice and the ice cold water with a blender. — Season with salt and cayenne pepper. Divide the hummus in 3 portions.

RED BEET HUMMUS

Cut the red beet into small pieces and add to the hummus. — Mix with a blender until creamy. Season with lemon juice, lemon zest, cumin, tahini, salt, and pepper.

Tip: The red beet develops its color and taste better when it is wrapped raw in aluminum foil and baked in the oven.

KALAMATA HUMMUS

Core the Kalamata olives and add together with the thyme leaves to the hummus and mix with a blender until creamy. — Season with lemon juice and lemon zest.

SERVE

Put the hummus in three different bowls and serve with olive oil and crispy Arabic bread.

Tip: For a green variation, puree fresh herbs and mix together with the hummus, season generously.

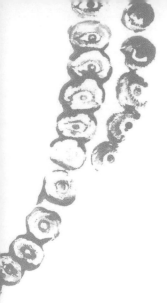

HIRSE-PARANUSS-TABOULEH
MILLET BRAZIL NUT TABBOULEH

ZUBEREITUNG

Die Hirse mit 2 EL Öl kurz andünsten und zusammen mit dem Wasser auf kochen. Auf kleiner Flamme ca. 15 Minuten köcheln lassen, bis die Hirse gar, aber immer noch leicht bissfest ist. Die Hirse 10 Minuten mit geschlossenem Deckel ruhen lassen. — Die Nüsse klein hacken und mit der Hirse vermengen. — Die Tomaten entkernen und in Würfel schneiden. Das Weiße und Hellgrüne der Frühlingszwiebeln in sehr feine Ringe schneiden. Die Blätter der Minze abzupfen und zusammen mit den Petersilienstängeln- und Blättern fein hacken. — Den Zitronensaft mit Olivenöl und etwas Salz und Pfeffer verrühren und alle Zutaten minteinander vermengen. Mit Salz abschmecken.

ZUM ANRICHTEN

Die Romanasalatblätter trennen und auf jedes Blatt etwas Hirse-Paranuss-Tabouleh verteilen und mit gehackten Nüssen servieren.

PREPARATION

Sauté the millet with 2 Tbsp. vegetable oil. Add water and bring to the boil. Simmer on low for approx. 15 minutes until al dente. Allow to rest for 10 minutes with the lid closed. — Chop the nuts and mix with the millet. — Remove the seeds of the tomatoes and cut into dices. Cut the white and green parts of the spring onions into very thin rings. Chop the mint leaves, parsley leaves, and thin parsley stems. Mix the lemon juice with the olive oil and season with salt and pepper. Mix all ingredients together and season with salt.

SERVE

Separate the romaine lettuce leaves and place the millet Brazil nut tabbouleh on each leaf and serve with chopped nuts.

LABNEH MIT SALSA CRIOLLA UND ARABISCHEM BROT
LABNEH WITH SALSA CRIOLLA AND ARABIC BREAD

LABNEH
Knoblauch mit Meersalz zu einer Paste zerdrücken (im Mörser oder mit einem Messer auf einem Brett). — Knoblauchsalzpaste zum Joghurt geben und sehr gut verrühren. — Ein großes Sieb mit einem Mulltuch auslegen und den Joghurt dazugeben. Das Sieb auf eine große Schüssel setzen, damit die Molke ablaufen kann und 24 Stunden abtropfen lassen. Falls die Masse noch zu flüssig ist, am nächsten Morgen mit den Händen leicht ausdrücken. Je länger dem Joghurt die Molke entzogen wird, desto fester wird der Frischkäse.

SALSA CRIOLLA
Karotte und Schalotte schälen und klein würfeln. Paprika und Chili entkernen und klein würfeln. Koriander mit Stängeln und der Wurzel klein hacken. Alles mit Limettensaft und Olivenöl vermengen und mit Salz, Pfeffer sowie Zucker abschmecken. Vor dem Servieren mindestens 10 Minuten ziehen lassen.

ARABISCHES BROT
Das arabische Brot in beliebig kleine Teile schneiden oder reißen, locker auf einem Backblech verteilen und mit 2 EL Sumak, 5 EL Olivenöl und 1/2 TL Salz bestreuen und kräftig mit dem Brot vermengen. Im vorgeheizten Ofen bei 180°C für 8 Minuten goldbraun backen.

ZUM ANRICHTEN
Labneh in eine Schüssel oder in Gläser füllen, Salsa Criolla hinzufügen und mit Olivenöl beträufeln. Mit knusprigem arabischen Brot servieren.

LABNEH
Grind the garlic with some sea salt and smash to a paste (in a mortar or with a knife on a cutting board). — Add the garlic salt paste to the yoghurt and mix well. — In a large sieve, line several layers of cheesecloth and pour the yoghurt on top. Place the sieve on a large bowl and allow to drain for 24 hours. If the mass is too wet on the next morning, squeeze the liquid out of the mass using your fingers. The longer the whey is removed, the firmer the cheese becomes.

SALSA CRIOLLA
Peel and cut the carrot into dices, finely chop the shallot. Remove the seeds of the pepper and chili and finely dice as well. Finely chop the coriander. Mix with lime juice and olive oil and season with salt, pepper, and sugar. Allow to rest for at least 10 minutes before serving.

ARABIC BREAD
Cut or tear the bread slices into small pieces and spread 2 slices each loosely on a baking tray. Sprinkle with 2 Tbsp. sumac, 5 Tbsp. olive oil and 1/2 tsp. salt and mix well. Bake in preheated oven at 180°C for 8 minutes until golden brown.

FOR SERVING
Place the labneh in a bowl or glass, add salsa criolla and sprinkle with olive oil. Serve with crispy Arabic bread.

HERZHAFTE SFIHA-VARIATIONEN

TEIG

Zucker und Hefe in ein Gefäß geben und in etwas lauwarmem Wasser auflösen. 5 Minuten ruhen lassen. Mehl, Salz, Hefemischung und Olivenöl in einer großen Schüssel vermengen. — Danach ca. 500 ml lauwarmes Wasser oder Milch hinzufügen, kräftig durchkneten, bis ein glatter Teig entsteht. — Den Teig mit einem Tuch abdecken und an einem warmen Ort mindestens 45 Minuten ruhen lassen. Das Volumen des Teigs sollte sich dabei in etwa verdoppeln. — Den Teig nochmals kurz durchkneten, ausrollen und mit einer runden Form (ø 10 cm) ausstechen. Mit genügend Abstand auf ein Blech mit Backpapier legen.

LAMMBELAG

Zwiebel in Würfel schneiden und die Blattpetersilie klein hacken. Die Tomaten entkernen und klein würfeln. Das Lammfleisch in einen Mixer geben zu einer feinen Konsistenz verarbeiten. — Lammfleisch, Zwiebeln, Petersilie, Tomaten, Zitronensaft und die Gewürze in eine Schüssel geben und miteinander vermengen. Mit Meersalz abschmecken.

SPINAT-FETA BELAG

Blattspinat waschen und abtrocknen. Knoblauch fein hacken. — In einer Pfanne das Öl mit dem Knoblauch kurz anschmoren, Spinat hinzufügen und dünsten, bis er zusammenfällt. Im Sieb abtropfen lassen und leicht ausdrücken. Mit Cayennepfeffer, Salz und Pfeffer abschmecken. — Feta trocken tupfen und zerkrümeln.

LACHSTARTAR

Den Lachs entgräten, waschen, trocken tupfen, klein hacken und kalt stellen. Die Schalotten schälen und in feine Würfel schneiden. Die Blattpetersilie mit dünnen Stängeln klein hacken und den Staudensellerie in kleine Würfel schneiden. Schalotten, Petersilie, Staudensellerie und Ingwer mit dem Fisch und dem Olivenöl vermengen und mit Salz, Pfeffer und etwas Tabasco würzen. Erst dann mit Zitronenabrieb und mit 1 EL Zitronensaft abschmecken.

GUACAMOLE

Avocado halbieren, entkernen und das Fruchtfleisch auslösen. In eine Schüssel füllen, mit Zitronensaft mischen und mit einer Gabel zerdrücken. — Schalotten schälen, die Chilischote entkernen und beides klein würfeln. Die Korianderstiele hacken. Die Tomaten aushöhlen, flach drücken und würfeln. Die Hälfte für die Dekoration beiseite legen. — Alle Zutaten miteinander vermengen und mit Salz und Pfeffer abschmecken. — Die Guacamole kalt stellen und später auf die Sfiha verteilen.

BACKEN

Backofen auf 220 °C vorheizen. — Auf 8 Sfihas jeweils 1 gehäuften EL Lammbelag mittig verteilen. — Backzeit ca. 15 Minuten. — Für die anderen Sfihas den Teig (ohne Belag) mit einer Gabel einstechen und auf mittlerer Schiene ca. 10 Minuten backen.

ZUM ANRICHTEN

Lamm-Sfihas: mit Granatapfelkernen und Petersilie garnieren. — Spinat-Sfihas: Spinat mittig verteilen und mit Feta bestreuen. — Guacamole-Sfihas: Guacamole verstreichen und mit den restlichen Tomatenwürfeln belegen. — Lachs-Sfihas: je 1 EL Tartar auf die Teiglinge geben.

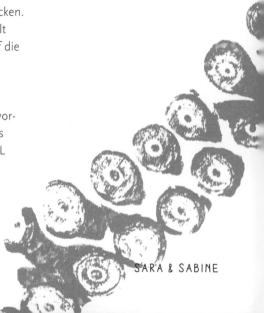

100

SAVORY SFIHA-VARIATIONS

DOUGH

Put sugar and yeast in a cup and dissolve in warm water. Let rest for 5 minutes. Put flour, salt, yeast mix and olive oil in a large bowl and mix. — Add approx. 500 ml of lukewarm water and knead well until smooth and soft. — Cover the dough with a kitchen towel and allow to rest in a warm place for at least 45 minutes. The volume of the dough should double in this time. — Knead the dough briefly again, roll out and cut out circles (ø 10 cm). Place the pizzas on a backing tray with proper distance.

LAMB TOPPING

Cut the onion into dices and chop the parsley. Hollow, core, and dice the tomatoes. Place the lamb into a blender and mix until fine consistency. — Put lamb, onions, parsley, tomatoes, lemon juice and the spices into a bowl and mix well. Season with sea salt.

SPINACH-FETA TOPPING

Wash the spinach and dry well. Finely chop the garlic. — In a pan, briefly sauté the garlic with some oil and add the spinach shortly after. Season with cayenne, salt and pepper. Dab dry the feta and crumble with a fork.

SALMON TARTAR TOPPING

Fillet, wash, dab dry, chop and refrigerate the salmon. Cut the shallot and the celery into small dices and finely chop the parsley. Mix the shallots, parsley, celery, ginger with the salmon and olive oil and season with salt, pepper and Tabasco. Only then, zest the lemon and season with 1 tsp. lemon juice.

GUACAMOLE TOPPING

Halve the avocado, remove the seed, smash the interior with a fork or potato masher and mix with lemon juice. — Peel the shallots, core the chili and cut both into small dices. Finely chop the coriander stems. Hollow the tomatoes, flatten, and cut into small dices. Set half of the cubes aside for garnish. — Mix all ingredients together and season with salt and pepper. — Refrigerate the guacamole and place on the Sfiha later.

BAKING

Preheat the oven at 220 °C. — Place 1 Tbsp. lamb topping in the center of 8 sfihas. — Bake for approx. 15 minutes. — For the sfihas that will be topped with salmon tartar, guacamole and spinach make little holes in the center of the pizzas with a fork. Bake for 10 minutes.

FOR SERVING

Lamb-sfihas: garnish with pomegranate seeds and parsley. — Spinach-sfihas: place spinach in the center and top with feta. — Guacamole-sfihas: put guacamole in the center and garnish with tomato cubes. — Salmon-sfihas: place 1 Tbsp. tartar on each sfiha.

1 Zucker und Hefe in lauwarmem Wasser auflösen und 5 Minuten ruhen lassen. Dissolve sugar and yeast in warm water, and let rest for 5 minutes. 2 Je länger der Teig geknetet wird, desto besser wird er. The longer the dough is being kneaded the softer it gets. 3 Teig ausrollen und mit einer runden Form ausstechen. Roll out the dough and cut out circles. 4 Ingwer verleiht dem Lachs Tartar eine besonders frische Note. Ginger gives the salmon tartar a particularly fresh note. 5 Ist noch frischer Labneh übrig? Ebenfalls eine gelungene Sfiha-Variante! Is there any fresh labneh left? Also a delicious sfiha-variation! 6 Gehackte Korianderstiele geben der Guacamole angenehme Frische. Chopped coriander stems add a delightful freshness to the guacamole. 7 Beim Belag der Sfihas sind der Kreativität keine Grenzen gesetzt – grüner Spargel schmeckt besonders gut. When it comes to topping the sfihas there is no limit in creativity – especially with green asparagus, it tastes delicious.

LIMONADE MIT ZITRONENGRAS
LEMONADE WITH LEMONGRASS

LIMONADE
Zitronen auspressen und
die Blätter der Minze
abzupfen. Zitronengras
putzen und in dicke
Scheiben schneiden. Zitronensaft, Minze, Zitro-
nengras und Ingwer mit
dem Wasser, braunem
Zucker und etwas Crushed
Ice mixen.

ZUM ANRICHTEN
Die Limonade durch ein
Sieb passieren und in
Gläser füllen. Mit Zitronen-
schnitzen dekorieren.

LEMONADE
Squeeze lemons and
pluck off the leaves
of mint. Cut the lemon
gras into thick pieces.
Mix lemon juice, mint,
lemongrass and gin-
ger with water, brown
sugar and a little
crushed ice.

FOR SERVING
Pass the lemonade
through a sieve
and pour into glas-
ses. Garnish with
lemon wedges.

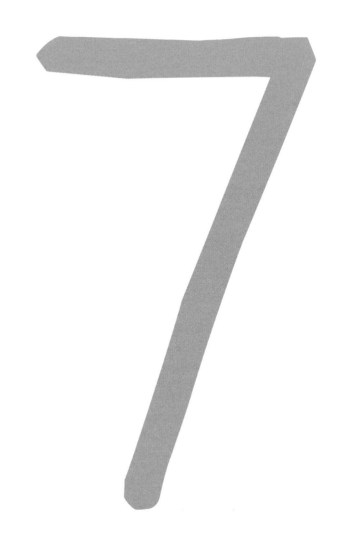

7

DREI-STERNE-PAKORAS
THREE-STAR PAKORAS

SIMI & DIEGO

Der Chefkoch Diego Muñoz, Peruaner und Mann von Welt, lädt ins Drei-Sterne-Restaurant Aqua nach Wolfsburg ein. In der Profiküche des Restaurants von Sven Elverfeld, jeder an seinem Herd, jeder vom anderen lernend, begegnen sich zwei Menschen, deren Leben sich schlicht ums Kochen dreht. Simi, eine Afghanin, Hindu und Frau von Welt, hat traditionelle Gerichte für die Begegnung ausgewählt. Gerichte, die sie mit ihrer Heimat verbindet. Seit ihrer Ankunft in Deutschland vor mehr als einem Jahr hat Simi sich bereits in kulinarische Experimente mit typisch deutschem Gemüse wie Rhabarber und Kohlrabi gestürzt. Tradition ist hier ein dehnbarer Begriff geworden. Für Diego ist vor allem der afghanische Reis, golden und langkörnig, eine Einladung zu Neuem. Der einfache Dip von Simi aus Minze, Koriander, Knoblauch und mit einem Hauch Chili überzeugt die gesamte Küchenmannschaft. Nach sehr erfolgreichen Jahren mit dem weltbekannten Spitzenrestaurant Astrid y Gastón in Lima – Rang 14 bei „The World's 50 Best Restaurants" im Jahr 2015 – ist Diego nun auf Reisen. Für das Kreieren neuer Rezepte und frischer Geschmacksideen ist Inspiration vonnöten. Die Koch-Begegnung in Wolfsburg ist damit ein Lob auf das Experimentieren. Mach mit, fang an, vielleicht sogar noch heute mit den Pakoras von Simi und Diego, die mindestens drei Sterne wert sind!

The head chef Diego Muñoz – Peruvian and citizen of the world – has invited us to the three-star restaurant Aqua in Wolfsburg. In the professional kitchen of Sven Elverfeld's restaurant two people meet whose lives revolve around cooking: each at their own stove, each learning from the other. Simi – Afghan, Hindu and citizen of the world – has prepared traditional dishes for this encounter, dishes that remind her of her home country. Since arriving in Germany over a year ago Simi has already thrown herself into culinary experiments with German ingredients such as rhubarb and kohlrabi. Tradition has therefore become a flexible term. Diego especially considers the Afghan rice, golden and long-grained, an invitation for discovering new culinary horizons. Simi's simple dip, made of mint, coriander, garlic and with a pinch of chili, fully convinces the whole kitchen team. After his very successful years in the world-famous restaurant Astrid y Gastón in Lima – ranked fourteenth in the "The World's 50 Best Restaurants" in 2015 – Diego is now traveling in search of inspiration for the creation of new recipes and flavors. The cooking encounter in Wolfsburg is thus an ode to experimentation. Join the delightful crossover, perhaps even today, with Simi's and Diego's pakoras which are worth at least three stars!

MENÜ

VORSPEISEN

KNUSPRIGE PAKORAS
MIT FRISCHEM DIP

AVOCADO
CAUSA MIT
HÜHNCHENFÜLLUNG

HAUPTSPEISE

AFGHANISCHER
GEMÜSEREIS
MIT GEBACKENER
LAMMKEULE

NACHSPEISE

SÜßE TEIGBÄLLCHEN
MIT FRISCHEN BEEREN

**KNUSPRIGE PAKORAS
MIT FRISCHEM DIP**

Für die Pakoras:
350 g Gemüse der Saison
250 g Kichererbsenmehl
1/2 TL Kurkuma
1/2 TL Chilipulver
1 TL Garam Masala
1 l Pflanzenöl zum Frittieren
280 ml Wasser
Salz

Für den Minz-Koriander Dip:
1 Bund Minze
1/2 Bund Koriander
2 Knoblauchzehen
1/2 TL Chilipulver
50 g Joghurt, 10 % Fett
Salz

**AVOCADO CAUSA
MIT HÜHNCHENFÜLLUNG**

Für den Teig:
500 g festkochende Kartoffeln
3 EL Rapsöl
1 EL Salz
1 Limette
100 g Ají Amarillo Paste

Für den Hühnchensalat:
250 g Hühnerbrust
1 Lorbeerblatt
100 g Mayonnaise
1 Limette
15 g gelbe Paprika
15 g grüne Paprika
15 g rote Paprika
1 mittelgroße Tomate
1/2 Bund Schnittlauch
Salz, Pfeffer

Zum Anrichten:
2 mittelgroße Avocados
1 Limette
6 Wachteleier

1 Hühnerei
etwas Mayonnaise
1/2 Bund Schnittlauch

**GEMÜSEREIS MIT
LAMMKEULE**

Für die Lammkeule:
1 Lammkeule (ca. 800 g)
1 Bund Thymian
1 Knolle Knoblauch
4 Schalotten
etwas Olivenöl
Salz, Pfeffer

Für den Reis:
350 g Basmatireis
4 Karotten
1 gelbe Paprika
1 grüne Paprika
1 Zwiebel
1 Knoblauchzehe
75 g Rosinen
50 g Cashewnüsse
50 g Mandeln
Pflanzenöl zum Frittieren
Butter zum Braten
2 TL Garam Masala
1 TL gemahlener Koriander

SÜßE TEIGBÄLLCHEN

Für die Teigbällchen:
200 g Milchpulver
50 g Mehl
1 EL Milch
1 Msp. Backpulver
Pflanzenöl zum Frittieren

Für den Zuckersirup:
250 g Zucker
250 ml Wasser
1 EL Rosenwasser
3 Kardamomkapseln

Zum Anrichten:
300 g Beeren der Saison

CRISPY PAKORAS WITH A FRESH DIP

For the pakoras:
350 g seasonal vegetables
250 g chickpea flour
1/2 tsp. turmeric powder
1/2 tsp. chili powder
1 tsp. garam masala
1 l vegetable oil for deep-frying
280 ml water
salt

For the mint-coriander dip:
1 bunch mint
1/2 bunch coriander
2 garlic cloves
1/2 tsp. chili powder
50 g yoghurt, 10 % fat
salt

AVOCADO CAUSA WITH CHICKEN FILLING

For the dough:
500 g waxy potato
3 Tbsp. canola oil
1 Tbsp. salt
1 lime
100 g Ají Amarillo paste

For the chicken salad:
250 g chicken breast
1 bay leaf
100 g mayonnaise
1 lime
15 g yellow bell pepper
15 g green bell pepper
15 g red bell pepper
1 medium-sized tomato
1/2 bunch chives
salt, pepper

For serving:
2 medium-sized avocados
1 lime
6 quail eggs

1 egg
some mayonnaise
1/2 bunch chives

VEGETABLE RICE WITH LEG OF LAMB

For the lamb:
1 leg of lamb (about 800 g)
1 garlic bulb
4 shallots
1 bunch thyme
some olive oil
salt, pepper

For the rice:
350 g basmati rice
4 carrots
1 yellow pepper
1 green pepper
1 onion
1 garlic clove
75 g raisins
50 g cashews
50 g almonds
vegetable oil for deep-frying
butter for frying
2 tsp. garam masala
1 tsp. ground coriander

SWEET MILKY BALLS

For the milky balls:
200 g milk powder
50 g flour
1 Tbsp. milk
1 pinch baking powder
vegetable oil for frying

For the syrup:
250 g sugar
250 ml water
1 Tbsp. rosewater
3 cardamom pods

For serving:
300 g seasonal berries

MENÜ
SERVES 4

———————

STARTERS

CRISPY PAKORAS WITH A FRESH DIP

AVOCADO CAUSA WITH TENDER CHICKEN FILLING

MAIN DISH

AFGHAN VEGETABLE RICE WITH BAKED LEG OF LAMB

DESSERT

SWEET MILKY BALLS WITH FRESH BERRIES

KNUSPRIGE PAKORAS MIT FRISCHEM DIP
CRISPY PAKORAS WITH A FRESH DIP

PAKORAS
Das Gemüse putzen, schälen und in mundgerechte Stücke schneiden. — Das Kichererbsenmehl in eine Schüssel geben, mit den Gewürzen vermischen und unter ständigem Rühren das Wasser hinzugeben. — Das Pflanzenöl in einer großen Pfanne erhitzen, 180°C in der Fritteuse. Das Öl hat die perfekte Temperatur, wenn man etwas Teig in das Öl hineingibt und dieser sofort beginnt zu frittieren. — Das Gemüse wird nun einzeln im Teig gewendet und für ca. 4–5 Minuten im Öl goldgelb ausgebacken.

MINZ-KORIANDER-DIP
Die Minze und den Koriander grob hacken und in einen Küchenmixer geben. Dazu die geschälten Knoblauchzehen sowie das Chilipulver geben und zusammen sehr fein pürieren. — Nun den Joghurt dazugeben und erneut mixen, bis eine cremige Masse entsteht. — Den Minz-Koriander Dip zusamen mit den knusprigen Pakoras servieren.

PAKORAS
Wash and peel vegetables and cut into bite-sized chunks. — In a bowl, mix the chickpea flour together with the spices and add 280 ml water, stirring throughout. — Heat up 1 l of vegetable oil in a pan. The oil has the perfect temperature when a little piece of batter immediately starts to deep-fry on contact. — Cover the vegetable chunks in the chickpea batter and deep-fry them for about 4–5 minutes or until golden brown.

MINT-CORIANDER DIP
Coarsely chop the mint and coriander and place in a kitchen blender. Add peeled garlic and the chili powder and finely blend together into a fine mixture. — Now add the yoghurt and blend again until the mass is creamy. Season with salt. — Serve the mint-coriander dip together with the pakoras.

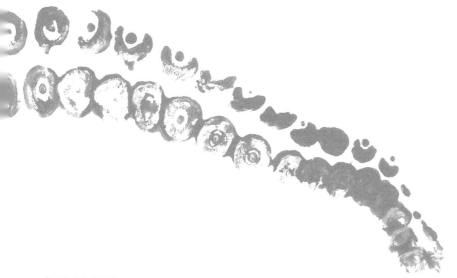

AVOCADO CAUSA MIT HÜHNCHENFÜLLUNG
AVOCADO CAUSA WITH CHICKEN FILLING

TEIG

Die Kartoffeln putzen und im Dampfkochtopf oder Ofen garen, schälen und zu einer trockenen Masse passieren. Die Limette pressen und den Saft auffangen. — Sobald die Kartoffeln abgekühlt sind, mit Salz, Rapsöl, Chilipaste sowie dem Limettensaft vermengen und durch eine Kartoffelpresse drücken, bis die Masse homogen und glatt ist. Bis zur Zubereitung an einem kühlen Ort aufbewahren.

HÄHNCHENSALAT

Etwas Wasser mit 1 TL Salz und dem Lorbeerblatt zum Kochen bringen. Darin die Hühnerbrust kochen, bis sie durchgegart und zart ist. — Abkühlen lassen und in feine Stücke zupfen. Paprika und Tomaten in sehr kleine Würfel schneiden. Die Limette heiß waschen und die Schale fein abreiben. Den Schnittlauch fein hacken. — Alle Zutaten in einer mittelgroßen Schüssel vermengen und mit Salz und Pfeffer würzen. Beiseitestellen.

ZUM ANRICHTEN

Die Limette auspressen und die geschälten Avocados damit einreiben, sodass sie nicht braun werden. Der Kern entfernen und in dünne Scheiben schneiden. — Den Schnittlauch fein hacken. — Die Wachteleier für 2 Minuten, das Hühnerei für 10 Minuten in kochendem Wasser garen, danach abschrecken und schälen. — Einmal abgekühlt, Eiweiß vom Eigelb trennen. Fein schneiden und beiseite stellen. — Die Kartoffelbreimasse auf einem mit Frischhaltefolie ausgelegtem Blech oder einem anderen glatten Untergrund ca. 1 cm dick ausbreiten. — Darauf zuerst die in dünne Scheiben geschnittenen Avocados und dann den Hähnchensalat geben. Mithilfe der Frischhaltefolie vorsichtig zu einer Causa rollen. Die überstehenden Ränder abschneiden und die Frischhaltefolie entfernen. — Zum Dekorieren der Causa Mayonnaise darüber geben, ein paar Scheiben Avocado, das in Scheiben geschnittene Eiweiß und Dotter. — Zum Schluss mit Schnittlauch und halbierten Wachteleiern garnieren.

DOUGH

Steam or bake the potatoes until they are cooked through. Peel them and pass through a food mill to form a dry mass. Allow to cool down. Meanwhile, juice the lime. — Once the potatoes are cold, mix with salt, canola oil, chili paste and lime juice, and pass through a food mill until the mixture is smooth. Keep cool until serving.

CHICKEN SALAD

At first, add a pinch of salt and 1 bay leaf to water and bring to the boil. — Add the chicken breast and allow to cook until tender. Leave to cool down and then pull into fine pieces. Chop peppers and tomatoes, and finely grate the peel of the lime. In a medium bowl, mix all ingredients together, season with salt and pepper until the salad is creamy and set aside.

FOR SERVING

Juice the lime and rub the juice over the pealed avocados to prevent browning. Remove the pip and cut the fruit pulp into thin slices. Finely chop the chives. — In a small saucepan, bring water to the boil and cook the quial eggs for 2 minutes, the other egg for 10 minutes. Afterwards, pour ice water over them and peel the eggs. — Once cooled, separate egg whites from yolks, cut finely and set aside. Spread the dough approx. 1 cm thick on cling film or a smooth surface. — Layer the finely sliced avocado, followed by the chicken salad on to the potato dough. Carefully roll everything together into a causa. Top the causa with some mayonnaise, a few slices of avocado, the sliced up egg yolk and egg white. — Finish everything with chives and half-cut quail eggs on top.

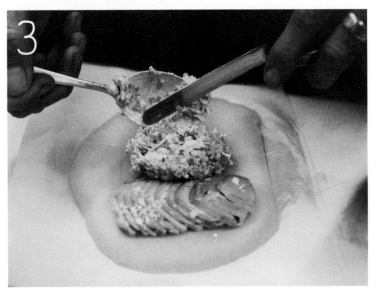

1 Die Kartoffelmasse durch eine Kartoffelpresse drücken, bis sie homogen und glatt ist. Pass the potato mixture through a food mill to form a smooth mass. 2 Die Avocados mit Limettensaft einreiben und in dünne Scheiben schneiden. Rub the peeled avocado with lime, and cut into thin slices. 3 Die Kartoffelbreimasse auf einem mit Frischhaltefolie ausgelegten Blech oder einem anderen glatten Untergrund ca. 1 cm dick ausbreiten. Avocadoscheiben und Hähnchensalat darauf verteilen. Spread the dough approx. 1 cm thick on cling film or a smooth surface. Layer the finely sliced avocado, followed by the chicken salad on to the potato dough. 4 Zu einer Causa rollen und mit gehacktem Schnittlauch garnieren. Roll into a causa and garnish with choped chives.

AFGHANISCHER GEMÜSEREIS MIT GEBACKENER LAMMKEULE
AFGHAN VEGETABLE RICE WITH BAKED LEG OF LAMB

LAMMKEULE

Die Lammkeule oben und unten etwas vom Knochen lösen. Die Schalotten schälen und in feine Streifen schneiden. Von unten wie folgt aufschichten: Zuerst Thymian, dann die Zwiebeln und dann die Lammkeule. Etwas Olivenöl darüber geben und mit Meersalz und Pfeffer würzen. Den Knoblauch halbieren und salzen. Mit Alufolie abdecken und neben der Keule platzieren, so gibt dieser nur ganz dezent seinen kräftigen Geschmack ab. Die Lammkeule im vorgeheizten Backofen bei 200 °C für 20 Minuten und bei 175 °C für 2,5 Stunden garen lassen, bis sich das Fleisch leicht vom Knochen lösen lässt.

REIS

Den Basmati Reis für ca. 3 Stunden in Wasser einlegen. Das Wasser 2–3 mal wechseln. — Die Karotten und die Paprika in feine Stifte schneiden. Zwiebel und Knoblauch hacken. Nüsse, Karotten und Paprika separat frittieren und danach auf einen Teller geben. — Reis abgießen. — Etwas Butter in einem Topf zerlassen und die Zwiebel und den Knoblauch dazu geben, den Reis 1 Minute mit anbraten. Dann das Wasser dazugeben und den Reis, wie auf der Verpackung angegeben, fertig garen. — Erst am Schluss mit den Gewürzen abschmecken.

ZUM ANRICHTEN

Den Reis auf einen großen Teller geben und dann nach und nach Nüsse, Rosinen, Karotten und Paprika Schicht für Schicht dazu geben. — Dann das Lammfleisch vom Knochen lösen und auf dem Reis verteilen.

LAMB

Loosen the meat a bit from the top and bottom of the bone. — Peel shallots and cut into fine strips. Layer from the bottom as followed: First thyme, then the shallots and then the leg of lamb. Drizzle a bit of olive oil over the top and sesaon with sea salt and pepper. — Cut the garlic bulb into halves and season with salt. Cover in aluminium foil and place it next to the meat for a soft garlic flavor. — Put the lamb in the preheated oven for 20 minutes at 200 °C and then cook for 2.5 hours at 175 °C until the meat can be easily removed from the bone.

RICE

Allow basmati rice to soak in water for 3 hours. Change the water 2–3 times throughout. — Peel the carrots and wash the peppers, then cut into thin sticks. Chop the onion and garlic. Deep-fry nuts, carrots and peppers individually and put on a separate plate. — Drain the rice. — Melt some butter in a pan and fry the chopped onions and garlic. Add the rice and fry together for 1 minute. Then add the water and cook the rice as indicated on the packaging. — At the end of the cooking process add the spices.

FOR SERVING

Place the rice on a large plate and then layer the nuts, raisins, carrots and peppers on top. — Then loosen the lamb meat from the bone and spread on the rice.

SÜßE TEIGBÄLLCHEN MIT FRISCHEN BEEREN
SWEET MILKY BALLS WITH FRESH BERRIES

MILCHBÄLLCHEN
Alle Zutaten für die Teigbällchen zu einer homogenen Masse vermengen und im Anschluss kleine Bällchen formen. Pflanzenöl in einer Pfanne erhitzen und die Bällchen darin frittieren, bis sie goldbraun sind.

SIRUP
Für den Sirup das Wasser und den Zucker zum Kochen bringen und einige Minuten köcheln lassen, bis eine klebrige Masse entsteht. Dann den Topf vom Herd nehmen und das Rosenwasser und die Kardamomkapseln hinzufügen.

ZUM ANRICHTEN
Die frittierten Bällchen in den Sirup legen und, sobald sie vollgesogen sind, mit frischen Beeren servieren.

MILKY BALLS
Mix all ingredients together to a smooth dough and form small balls from the mass. Heat vegetable oil in a pan and deep-fry them until golden brown.

SYRUP
For the syrup, in a small pot bring water and sugar to the boil and let simmer for a few minutes until it becomes a sticky mass. Turn the heat off and add the rosewater and the cardamom pods.

FOR SERVING
Place the deep-fried balls in the syrup and allow to soak up all liquid. Serve with fresh berries.

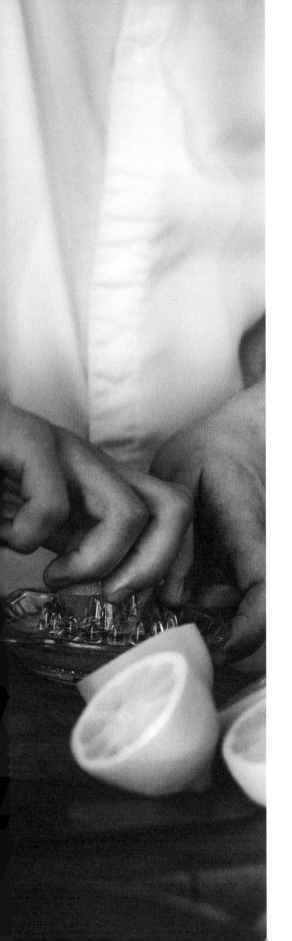

HAUTE CUISINE
À LA SYRIENNE

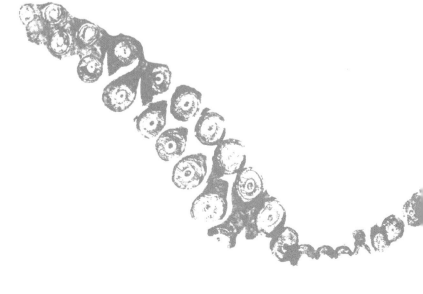

MZKIN & WILFRIED

Vor seinem Umzug nach Deutschland befürchtete Wilfried, Koch der französischen Botschaft in Berlin, es werde hier schlechter um die Küche stehen als in Frankreich mit seiner berühmten Haute Cuisine. Man esse hastig und nehme sich weniger Zeit für den Genuss, den gutes Essen bedeuten kann. Auch Mzkin empfindet die deutsche Küche als sehr einfach. In Syrien werde immer stundenlang gekocht und das gemeinsame Essen habe einen hohen Stellenwert. So treffen sich diese beiden Köche im lustvollen Zelebrieren des Kochens und Essens. Im Hintergrund läuft entspannte Musik und die beiden Enthusiasten einigen sich auf eine leicht abgewandelte syrische Vorspeise, einen Hauptgang aus Hühnchen mit „Pomme Anna" und einer syrischen Mandi-Sauce und auf eine ganz klassische französische Nachspeise. Fusion wird hier von Tradition eingerahmt. In der französischen Botschaft wird Mzkin schon bald Falafel zubereiten, Wilfrieds Lieblingsgericht der arabischen Küche. So geht das französisch-syrische Kochprojekt in eine weitere Runde: to be continued.

Before moving to Germany, Wilfried, chef at the French embassy in Berlin, was concerned that the German cuisine would be in a lot worse condition than the famous Haute Cuisine in France. People eating in a hurry, taking less time for the pleasures to be found in good food. Similarly Mzkin perceives the German cuisine to be very simple, whereas cooking in Syria often takes hours and eating together is an essential activity. Thus the two cooks bond over their passion for celebrating cooking and eating. With relaxing music playing in the background, the two enthusiasts quickly agree on a traditional but slightly modified Syrian starter, a main course of chicken and "Pomme Anna" with a Syrian mandi sauce and a classic French dessert. Here fusion is framed by tradition. Soon Mzkin will prepare falafel in the French embassy, Wilfried's favorite dish of Arabic cuisine. That way the French-Syrian cooking project enters the next round: to be continued.

MENÜ

VORSPEISE

WEINBLÄTTER GEFÜLLT MIT AROMATISCHEM COUSCOUS

HAUPTSPEISE

ZARTE HÜHNCHEN-ROULADEN AN „POMME ANNA"

NACHSPEISE

ZITRONENTARTE

WEINBLÄTTER GEFÜLLT MIT AROMATISCHEM COUSCOUS

16 Weinblätter aus dem Glas
250 g Couscous
2 EL Ghee
3 Schalotten
1 Knoblauchzehe
1 Zitrone
1 Karotte
1 Chili
50 g Walnusskerne, gehackt
1 Prise Kurkuma
1 EL frische Minze, gehackt
Salz
Pfeffer

ZARTE HÜHNCHEN-ROULADEN

Für die Hühnchenrouladen:
4 Hühnerbrüste
4 rote Paprika

Für die Mandi-Sauce:
2 rote Spitzpaprika
1 Zwiebel
2 Tomaten
1 *Handvoll* frischer Koriander
Salz
Pfeffer

Für die Zucchini-Sauce:
5 Zucchini
Salz

Für die Kartoffeln à la „Pomme Anna":
5 Kartoffeln
50 g Butter
Salz
Pfeffer

ZITRONENTARTE

Für die Zitronencreme:
200 ml Zitronensaft
4 Eier
150 g Butter
160 g Zucker
5 Gelatineblätter

Für den französischen Biskuitboden:
175 g Butter
140 g Mehl
70 g Zucker
25 g gemahlene Mandeln
2 g Salz
25 g Eigelb

GRAPE LEAVES FILLED WITH SAVORY COUSCOUS

16 grape leaves from a jar
250 g couscous
3 shallots
1 garlic clove
1 lemon
1 carrot
1 chili
50 g walnuts, chopped
1 pinch of turmeric
1 Tbsp. fresh mint, chopped
salt
pepper

TENDER CHICKEN ROLLS

For the chicken rolls:
4 chicken breasts
4 red bell peppers

For the mandi sauce:
2 red bell peppers
1 onion
2 tomatoes
1 handful of fresh coriander
salt
pepper

For the zucchini sauce:
5 zucchinis
salt

For the potatoes à la "Pomme Anna":
5 potatoes
50 g butter
salt
pepper

LEMON TART

For the lemon mousse:
200 ml lemon juice
4 eggs
150 g butter
160 g sugar
5 gelatin leaves

For the French sponge cake:
175 g butter
140 g flour
70 g sugar
25 g almond flour
2 g salt
25 g egg yolk

MENUE
SERVES 4

———————

STARTER

GRAPE LEAVES FILLED WITH SAVORY COUSCOUS

MAIN DISH

TENDER CHICKEN ROLLS WITH "POMME ANNA"

DESSERT

LEMON TART

WEINBLÄTTER GEFÜLLT
MIT AROMATISCHEM COUSCOUS
GRAPE LEAVES FILLED
WITH SAVORY COUSCOUS

WEINBLÄTTER
Die Weinblätter vorsichtig aus dem Glas holen, Stiele abschneiden und die Blätter kurz blanchieren.

COUSCOUS
Die Schalotten sehr fein hacken und in 2 EL Ghee sautieren, bis sie leicht braun gefärbt sind. Im Anschluss den gehackten Knoblauch hinzugeben und für 1 Minute mitbraten und dann von der Herdplatte nehmen. — Die Schale einer Zitrone abreiben, die Karotte ganz fein hobeln und beides separat aufbewahren. Die Chili fein hacken und zu den Schalotten geben. — Den Couscous mit den Walnusskernen langsam in einer Eisenpfanne rösten, bis er hellbraun ist und dann in eine zusätzliche Schale geben. Nun den Zwiebeln-Knoblauch-Chili Mix unter den Couscous heben, Kurkuma hinzufügen und alles gut vermengen. Die Zitronenzeste dazugeben und mit 300 ml kochendem Wasser aufgießen. Den Couscous nach ca. 1,5 Minuten einmal umrühren und am Schluss die geraspelte Karotte dazugeben, mit Salz und Pfeffer abschmecken und mit frischer Minze garnieren.

ZUM ANRICHTEN
Man isst dieses Gericht normalerweise mit den Händen. Dafür legt man ein Weinblatt in die Hand, platziert etwas Couscous darauf und genießt es!

WINE LEAVES
Take grape leaves carefully out of the jar, cut the stems and briefly blanch.

COUSCOUS
Finely chop the shallots and sauté with 2 Tbsp. ghee until light brown. Add the chopped garlic, fry for 1 minute, and then set aside. Finely grate the lemon peel and the carrot. — Chop the chili and add to the shallots. Slowly roast the chopped walnuts and the couscous in an iron pan until golden and set aside. Fold in the shallot-garlic-chili mix, the lemon zest and a pinch of curcuma and mix well. Now pour 300 ml boiling water and mix everything for 1.5 minutes. Before serving, add the carrots, season with salt and pepper and garnish with fresh mint leaves.

FOR SERVING
This dish is traditionally eaten with fingers. In order to do this, place one wine leaf in the middle of your hand, scoop a small ball of couscous with some grated carrot, lemon and mint on top, and roll it up.

ZARTE HÜHNCHENROULADEN AN „POMME ANNA"
TENDER CHICKEN ROLLS WITH "POMME ANNA"

HÜHNCHENROULADEN
Wenn vorhanden, die Haut der Hühnerbrüste entfernen und dann die Hühnerbrüste zwischen 2 Backpapierblätter legen. Bei 180°C für 30 Minuten im Backofen garen, bis sie knusprig sind. — Die Hühnerbrust aufschneiden und zwischen zwei Lagen Frischhaltefolie flach klopfen. — Die Paprika im vorgeheizten Backofen bei 220°C für 5–10 Minuten grillen, schälen und in Streifen schneiden. Dann auf die Hühnerbrust legen und mithilfe von Frischhaltefolie zu einer Roulade einrollen. Diese gefüllten Hühnerbrustrollen für ca. 20 Minuten bei 70° im Backofen garen; so verlieren sie später nicht ihre Form. Im Anschluss Folie entfernen und in einer Pfanne von beiden Seiten goldbraun anbraten.

MANDI-SAUCE
Die Paprika, Zwiebeln und Tomaten grob schneiden und anschließend sehr fein pürieren. — Den Koriander fein hacken, hinzugeben und mit Salz und Pfeffer abschmecken.

ZUCCHINI-SAUCE
Für die Sauce wird nur die Schale der Zucchini benötigt. — Dazu die Zucchini schälen und die Schale kurz in kochendem Wasser blanchieren. — Dann in kaltem Wasser abschrecken, pürieren und mit etwas Salz würzen.

KARTOFFELN À LA „POMME ANNA"
Die Kartoffeln in ca. 2 mm dünne Scheiben schneiden. — Für einige Minuten in kaltes Wasser legen, damit sie etwas an Stärke verlieren. Danach gut abtropfen lassen. — Eine Kastenform mit Backpapier auslegen und die Kartoffelscheiben darin aufschichten. — Die Butter schmelzen, mit Salz und Pfeffer würzen und die Kartoffelscheiben damit übergießen. — Die Kartoffeln bei 160°C für 40 Minuten im Backofen garen. — In der Kastenform über Nacht abkühlen lassen, am nächsten Tag in die gewünschte Portionsgröße schneiden und in einer Pfanne anbraten. Die krosse Kartoffelvariation zusammen mit den Dips und den zarten Hühnchenrouladen servieren.

CHICKEN ROLLS
Peel off the skin from the chicken breasts, and place between 2 baking sheets. Cook in the oven at 180°C for 30 minutes or until crispy. — Slice the chicken breasts open, place between 2 layers of cling film and pound them until flat. Put peppers in the oven at 220°C for 5–10 minutes to allow for peeling, then cut them into thin slices. Place sliced up red bell peppers on top of the chicken breasts and roll them up into a roulade. Cook in the oven at 70°C for 20 minutes to keep their form. Then remove the cling film and roast in a pan until golden brown.

MANDI SAUCE
Coarsely chop peppers, onion and tomatoes, and then blend them together. — Finely chop the coriander, add to the pureed pepper mix and season with salt and pepper.

ZUCCHINI SAUCE
For the sauce, only the zucchini peel is needed. In order to do so, peel the zucchini and briefly blanch the peel in boiling water. — Place immediately into a bowl of ice water to stop the cooking process and puree them. Season with salt.

POTATOES À LA "POMME ANNA"
Cut potatoes into approx. 2 mm thick slices. — Place for a few minutes in cold water to allow for the removal of excess starch, then drain well. — Line a loaf pan with baking paper and layer the potato slices into it. — Melt the butter, season with salt and pepper and pour it over the potato slices. — Bake potatoes in the oven at 160°C for 40 minutes. — Allow the potatoes to cool overnight. The following day, cut the desired portion size and fry in a pan. — Serve the crispy potato variation along with the dips and the tender chicken rolls.

ZITRONENTARTE
LEMON TART

ZITRONENCREME
Gelatine in kaltes Wasser legen. — In einer Schüssel über einem Wasserbad die Eier mit dem Zucker und dem Zitronensaft aufschlagen. — Anschließend die Gelatine und die weiche Butter hinzugeben und vermengen. — Die Creme über Nacht kalt stellen und später mit dem Spritzbeutel auf den Biskuitboden geben.

BISKUITBODEN
Alle Zutaten zu einem Teig verarbeiten und für einige Minuten stehen lassen. — Den Teig in die gewünschte Form geben und bei 175°C ca. 20 Minuten backen.

LEMON MOUSSE
Allow gelatin leaves to swell in cold water. — Whisk the eggs together with the sugar and the lemon juice in a double boiler over low heat. — Add the soft butter and soaked gelatin and mix thoroughly. — Allow to cool in the fridge. — Once cooled, top the French sponge cake with this mixture using an icing bag.

FRENCH SPONGE CAKE
Mix together all ingredients and let sit for a few minutes. — Pour dough in the desired form and bake at 175°C for 20 minutes.

KAFFEE TRADITIONEN
COFFEE TRADITIONS

In den arabischen Kulturen spielen Kaffee, aber auch schwarzer Tee und frischer Minztee eine wichtige Rolle. In Syrien etwa gehört vor allem Kaffee zur Lebensart und wird zu allen wichtigen Gelegenheiten serviert: von der Eheschließung über Reinigungsrituale bis hin zu Beerdigungen. Kaffee, auf Arabisch kahwa genannt, entspricht in der Region der türkischen Kaffeevariante: braun, zähflüssig und stark. Er wird in einer speziellen Kanne (dallah) auf dem Herd aufgebrüht und aus einer kleinen Tasse ohne Henkel (finjaan) getrunken. In Syrien wird nach dem Aufstehen zuerst Kaffee getrunken, beim Frühstück selbst dann schwarzer Tee. Häufig wird dem Kaffee Kardamom hinzugefügt, die Zugabe von Zucker ist abhängig vom individuellen Geschmack. Der Gedanke, dem Kaffee Milch hinzuzufügen, erscheint dem Liebhaber türkischen bzw. arabischen Kaffees ziemlich absurd.

Vor allem zu besonderen Gelegenheiten wie Hochzeiten und Beerdigungen wird der Kaffee extra heiß und kräftig genossen. Syrische Kaffeeliebhaber nehmen die Tasse in die rechte Hand und die Kanne immer in die linke. Vor allem ist darauf zu achten, die kleinen Tassen nicht bis zum Rand mit Kaffee zu füllen, denn dies wird als Zeichen verstanden, dass man die Person, der man gerade einschenkt, nicht mag. Wenn man seinen Kaffee ausgetrunken hat, schüttelt man die Tasse kurz oder gibt ein Handzeichen, sonst wird stetig nachgefüllt. Abhängig von der Region wird zum Kaffee etwas Süßes serviert. In der Golf-Region etwa gehören Datteln zum Kaffee dazu.

In Arab culture, coffee as well as black tea and fresh mint tea play an important role. In Syria, for example, coffee in particular is an important part of everyday life and is also served on special occasions: from weddings to cleaning rituals and funerals. Arabic coffee, or kahwa, is similar to its Turkish variant: brown, thick and strong. It is brewed in a special pot (dallah) on a stove and served in a small cup without a handle (finjaan). In Syria, one usually drinks coffee first thing in the morning, while breakfast itself is accompanied by black tea. Often cardamom is added, as well as sugar, depending on individual taste. The idea of adding milk to your coffee, however, seems quite absurd to lovers of Turkish or Arabic coffee.

Particularly on special occasions like weddings and funerals, coffee is served especially hot and strong. Syrian coffee lovers always hold the cup in their right hand and pour from the pot with their left. Most importantly, the small cup should not be filled with coffee to its brim, as this is seen as an insult to the person being served. Once one has had their fill, one quickly shakes the cup or gives a brief hand signal; otherwise the cup will constantly be refilled. Often, something sweet is served with the coffee, and this varies from region to region. In the Gulf region, for example, the coffee ritual is incomplete without dates.

9

PISTAZIEN UND NÜSSE
FÜR 1001 NACHT

PISTACHIOS AND NUTS
FOR 1001 NIGHTS

GHAITH & SVEN

Hier präsentieren wir ein märchenhaftes Menü aus Wolfsburg: Jakobsmuschel mit Apfelcouscous und einer Pistazien-Nuss-butter, Gewürztaube an bunten Linsen und syrischen Bohnen und Kartoffeln sowie ein Ayransorbet mit Dattelmousse und in Orangensaft eingelegten Kichererbsen. Chapeau! Ghaith und Sven haben schlicht gezaubert. Ausgehend von den syrischen Gerichten und ihren Zutaten haben die beiden Köche eine herrliche Menüfolge kreiert. Die Inspiration für solche Kreationen bekommt Sven fernab des Arbeitsplatzes und der Routine, gerne auch auf Reisen. So ist er nach Stationen in Japan, auf Kreta und in Dubai nun in Wolfsburg tätig und sammelt Sterne. Je fremder die Küchen, die er auf seinen Reisen kennenlernt, desto inspirierender. Auch Ghaith aus Aleppo hat inzwischen im Jemen und nun in Deutschland kulinarische Erfahrungen gesammelt. Sein Lieblingsgericht? Germknödel. Wir vermuten jedoch, dass der Knödel seine Spitzenposition in Ghaiths persönlicher Rangliste nur schwer wird halten können, denn die Konkurrenz dieses fulminanten Menüs ist überwältigend und wird der Drei-Sterne-Küche von Svens Restaurant gerecht. Besser geht kaum. Noch nicht mal in Tausendundeine Nacht.

We proudly present a magical menu from Wolfsburg: apple couscous with scallops and a pistachio-nut-butter, seasoned pigeon on a bed of colorful lentils and Syrian beans and potatoes, followed by an Ayran sorbet with date mousse and chickpeas marinated in orange juice. Chapeau! Ghaith and Sven conjured a simply fantastic meal. Inspired by the Syrian cuisine and its ingredients, the two chefs have created a wonderful menu. For such creations, Sven collects his inspirations far away from his work place and the usual routine, preferably when traveling the world. Currently, after cooking in Japan, on Crete and in Dubai, he finds himself in Wolfsburg, collecting Michelin stars. Indeed, the more exotic the cuisine, the more inspiring it is for Sven. Ghaith from Aleppo, too, has already gained culinary experiences in Yemen and Germany. His favorite dish? Jam-filled yeast dumplings. But after this meal, we guess, it will be hard for them to keep their top position in Ghaith's personal ranking. This brilliant menu is absolutely overwhelming and does more than satisfy Sven's three-star cuisine. It could not be any better. Not even in One Thousand and One Nights.

MENÜ

FÜR 4 PERSONEN

VORSPEISE

JAKOBSMUSCHELN MIT NUSSBUTTER AN APFELCOUSCOUS

HAUPTSPEISE

ORIENTALISCHE GEWÜRZTAUBE AN BEILAGENVARIATIONEN

NACHSPEISE

AYRANSORBET AN DATTELCREME

JAKOBSMUSCHELN MIT NUSSBUTTER AN APFELCOUSCOUS

Für die Jakobsmuscheln:
4 Jakobsmuscheln in der Schale
Olivenöl
Salz
weißer Pfeffer

Für die Pistazien-Nussbutter:
200 g Butter
40 g Pistazien, geraspelt
75 g Haselnüsse, geraspelt
1 TL Estragon
1 TL Kerbel
1 EL Zitronensaft
1 Knoblauchzehe
3 TL Petersilie
100 ml Gemüsebrühe

Für den Apfelcouscous:
150 g Couscous
2 EL Olivenöl
1 große Schalotte
150 ml Hühnerfond
1/2 Apfel
150 ml Apfelsaft
1 Anisstern
1 Prise Zimt
1 EL Arganöl
1 EL Zitronenöl
1 TL Zitronensaft
2 EL Blattpetersilie
Salz
weißer Pfeffer

ORIENTALISCHE GEWÜRZTAUBE AN BEILAGENVARIATIONEN

Für das Taubengewürz-Öl:
50 ml Olivenöl
5 ml Zitronenöl
5 ml Sesamöl
40 ml Arganöl

1/2 Anisstern
1/2 Lorbeerblatt
3 schwarze Pfefferkörner
2 Kardamomkapseln
1/4 Zimtstange
1/2 TL Kreuzkümmel
1/2 Knoblauchzehe

Für die Fladenbrotbrösel:
125 g Fladenbrot
Zitronenöl
Arganöl
1/2 EL Pistaziengrieß
Linsen-Gewürzmischung

Für die Taubenbrüste:
2 Etouffé-Tauben à 550 g
40 ml Gewürzöl
Salz
weißer Pfeffer
1/2 Thymianzweig
1/2 Rosmarinzweig
1/2 Knoblauchzehe
Butterschmalz

Für die Linsen:
1/2 Schalotte
1 rote Peperoni
Sesamöl
250 ml Gemüsefond
25 g gelbe Linsen
25 g rote Linsen
25 g Belugalinsen
25 g Puy-Linsen
25 g Berglinsen
2 Korianderstängel ohne Blätter

Für die Linsen-Gewürzmischung:
1 TL Raz el hanout
1 TL Mumbai Curry
1 EL Sumak
1 EL Purple Curry
1 Msp. Zimtpulver
1 Msp. Kurkuma

Für die grünen Bohnen:
300 g grüne Bohnen
1 Zwiebel
1 große Tomate
2 Knoblauchzehen
1 TL Kreuzkümmel
1 EL Tomatenmark
250 ml Gemüsefond
Salz
1 Msp. Zimt

Für die Korianderkartoffeln:
600 g Kartoffeln
5 Knoblauchzehen
1 EL Koriandersamen
50 g frischer Koriander
Olivenöl

AYRANSORBET AN DATTEL-CREME

Für das Ayransorbet:
500 g Joghurt, 10% Fett
200 ml Wasser
10 g Salz
20 g Zitrone
25 g Zucker

Für die Dattelcreme:
250 g Datteln
200 ml Orangensaft
100 ml Blutorangensaft
Abrieb von 1 Zitrone
1/2 Vanilleschote

Für das Kichererbsenpüree:
150 g Kichererbsen, eingeweicht
1 EL Butter
40 ml Pernod
450 ml Orangensaft
1/2 TL Cumin
1 Zimtstange
Abrieb von 1/2 Zitrone
100 g Zucker

SCALLOPS WITH NUT BUTTER AND APPLE COUSCOUS

For the scallops:
4 scallops in a shell
olive oil
salt
white pepper

For the pistachio-nut-butter:
200 g butter
40 g pistachios, grated
75 g hazelnuts, grated
1 tsp. tarragon, grated
1 tsp. chervil
1 Tbsp. lemon juice
1 garlic clove
3 tsp. parsley, chopped
100 ml vegetable stock

For the apple couscous:
150 g couscous
2 Tbsp. olive oil
1 shallot, finely chopped
150 ml chicken stock
3 Tbsp. apple, finely chopped cubes
150 ml apple juice
1 star anise
1 pinch of cinnamon
1 Tbsp. argan oil
1 Tbsp. lemon oil
1 tsp. lime juice
2 Tbsp. parsley, finely chopped
salt
white pepper

ORIENTAL PIGEON WITH SIDE DISH VARIATIONS

For the spiced oil:
50 ml olive oil
5 ml lemon oil
5 ml sesame oil
40 ml argan oil
1/2 star anis
1/2 bay leave
3 black peppercorns
2 cardamom capsules
1/4 cinnamon stick
1/2 tsp. cumin
1/2 garlic clove

For the flatbread crumbs:
125 g flat bread
lemon oil
argan öl
1/2 Tbsp. pistachio semolina
lentil spice mix

For the pigeon:
2 pieces Etouffé pigeon à 550 g
40 ml spiced oil
salt
white pepper
1/2 rosemary twig
1/2 thyme twig
1/2 garlic clove
clarified butter

For the lentils:
1/2 shallot
1 red pepper
sesame oil
250 ml vegetable stock
25 g yellow lentils
25 g red lentils
25 g beluga lentils
25 g puy lentils
25 g mountain lentils
2 coriander stems without leaves

For the lentil spice mix:
1 tsp. raz el hanout
1 tsp. Mumbai curry
1 Tbsp. sumac
1 Tbsp. purple curry
1 pinch of cinnamon
1 pinch of curcuma

For the green beans:
300 g green beans
1 onion
1 big tomato
2 garlic cloves
1 tbs. cumin
1 Tbsp. tomato paste
250 ml vegetable stock
salt
1 pinch of cinnamon

For the coriander potatoes:
600 g potatoes
5 garlic cloves
1 Tbsp. coriander seeds
50 g fresh coriander
olive oil

AYRAN SORBET WITH DATE CREAM

For the Ayran sorbet:
500 g yoghurt, 10% fat
200 ml water
10 g salt
20 g lemon
25 g sugar

For the date cream:
250 g dates
200 ml orange juice
100 ml red orange juice
lemon zest of 1 lemon
1/2 vanilla stick

For the chickpea mousse:
150 g chickpeas, soaked
1 Tbsp. butter
40 ml Pernod
450 ml orange juice
1/2 tbs. cumin
1 cinnamon stick
lemon zest of 1/2 lemon
100 g sugar

MENUE

STARTER

SCALLOPS WITH
NUT BUTTER
AND APPLE COUSCOUS

MAIN DISH

ORIENTAL PIGEON
WITH SIDE
DISH VARIATIONS

DESSERT

AYRAN SORBET WITH
DATE CREAM

GHAITH & SVEN

JAKOBSMUSCHELN MIT NUSSBUTTER AN APFELCOUSCOUS
SCALLOPS WITH NUT BUTTER AND APPLE COUSCOUS

JAKOBSMUSCHELN
Die Jakobsmuscheln mit einem stumpfen Küchenmesser aus der Schale herauslösen, Muskel und Innereien entfernen. Muschel kurz wässern und abtrocknen. Zum Servieren salzen und pfeffern und in Olivenöl glasig braten.

PISTAZIEN-NUSSBUTTER
Knoblauch in feine Scheiben schneiden. Mit einem Messer und etwas Salz zu einer Paste zerdrücken. Estragon und Kerbel in feine Streifen schneiden und Petersilie fein hacken. — Die Butter langsam schmelzen, mit den Haselnüssen und den Pistazien vermengen, Zitronensaft und Knoblauchpaste zugeben und abkühlen lassen. Die Kräuter hinzufügen, mit Salz und Pfeffer abschmecken und kalt stellen. — Zum Servieren Gemüsebrühe erhitzen und die Butter in kleinen Mengen nach und nach einrühren.

APFELCOUSCOUS
Die Schalotte fein schneiden und in Olivenöl unter ständigem Rühren glasig garen lassen. Den Couscous dazugeben und anschwitzen. Im Anschluss Apfelwürfel, Sternanis, Zimtpulver, Arganöl, Zitronenöl und Zitronensaft zugeben und mit der heißen Brühe ablöschen. Apfelsaft hinzufügen, kurz köcheln lassen und dabei rühren. Vom Herd nehmen und mit Klarsichtfolie abdecken. Den Couscous 15 Minuten quellen lassen und anschließend mit einem Schneebesen durchrühren. Er sollte locker und körnig sein. Zuletzt die Blattpetersilie zugeben und mit Salz und Pfeffer abschmecken.

ZUM ANRICHTEN
Die gebratenen Jakobsmuscheln auf dem Apfelcouscous platzieren und mit der Pistazien-Nussbutter nappieren.

SCALLOPS
Remove the scallops from their shells with a blunt kitchen knife and discard the muscle and the innards. Water and dry the shell. Before serving, season with salt and pepper and fry in olive oil.

PISTACHIO-NUT-BUTTER
Finely slice the garlic, add some salt and pepper and grind into a paste. — For the pistachio-nut-butter, melt the butter and mix it with finely chopped hazelnuts and pistachios, add lemon and garlic paste and allow to cool down. Add the herbs and season with salt and pepper. Leave to cool down. Heat the vegetable stock and slowly add to the butter in small amounts.

APPLE COUSCOUS
Finely chop and fry the shallots in olive oil until they are glassy in appearance. Add the couscous to the shallots and sauté. Add the apple cubes, star anise, cinnamon, argan oil, lemon oil and lemon juice and cook gently with 150 ml of chicken stock. Add apple juice and leave to simmer, stirring occasionally. Remove the pot from the heat and cover with plastic wrap. Let the couscous swell for 15 minutes, then stir with a whisk. The couscous should be loose and grainy. Finally, add the parsley and season with salt and pepper.

FOR SERVING
Place the fried scallops on the apple couscous and nap with pistachio-nut-butter.

ORIENTALISCHE GEWÜRZTAUBE
AN BEILAGENVARIATIONEN

TAUBENGEWÜRZ-ÖL
Oliven-, Zitronen-, Sesam-
und Arganöl erwärmen und
Gewürze zugeben. In ein
Gefäß füllen und ca. eine
Woche durchziehen lassen.
(Das Öl hält sich gut ver-
schlossen, kühl und dunkel
gelagert ca. 2 Wochen.)

LINSEN-GEWÜRZ-
MISCHUNG
Alle Zutaten vermengen
und beiseite stellen.

FLADENBROTBRÖSEL
Das Fladenbrot entrinden
und in dünne Scheiben
schneiden, mit etwas Öl
beträufeln und im Ofen
bei 150°C ca.15 Minuten
goldgelb backen. Danach
in einem Vakuumbeutel
(oder Gefrierbeutel) mit Hil-
fe eines Fleischklopfers
nicht zu fein klopfen.Die
entstandenen Brösel mit etwas Öl, dem Pistazien-
grieß, sowie der Gewürzmischung abschmecken.
(Die Brösel halten sich gut
verschlossen, kühl und
trocken gelagert ca.2 Wo-
chen und bieten sich
sehr gut für diverse Fleisch-
gerichte an.)

TAUBE
Die Taubenbrüste von der
Karkasse auslösen und die
Haut entfernen. Einzeln
mit je 10 ml Gewürzöl va-
kuumieren. — Die Beutel
mit den Taubenbrüsten
8 Minuten bei 64,8°C im
Wasserbad garen. Zum
Ruhen ca. 20 Minuten im
Wärmeschrank lagern.
Die Taubenbrüste aus den
Beuteln nehmen und
das Öl abschütten. An-
schließend in der geklärten
Butter mit den Kräutern
und dem Knoblauch von
beiden Seiten kurz nachbra-
ten. Aus der Pfanne
nehmen und auf einem
Küchenkrepp abfetten las-
sen. Mit Salz und Pfeffer
würzen.

*Tipp: Das Fleisch kann man
sich gleich beim Einkauf
vom Metzger vakuumieren
lassen. Auf Wunsch schwei-
ßen sie sicher auch ein
paar mitgebrachte Kräuter
und Gewürze mit ein!*

LINSEN
Die Linsen alle separat am
Vortag einweichen. —
Die Schalotte schälen und
mit einer Hälfte der
Peperoni grob klein schneiden, in etwas Sesamöl
anschwitzen, mit dem Ge-
müsefond aufkochen
und erkalten lassen. —
Linsen abpassieren und
sortenrein mit dem
ebenfalls abpassierten,
gut gesalzenen Gemüse-
fond ca. 2–8 Minuten
(gelbe und rote Linsen je
ca. 2 Minuten, die
übrigen Linsen je ca. 6–8
Minuten) kochen. —
Die zweite Hälfte der Peperoni in Brunoise (sehr
feine Würfel) schneiden,
kurz in kochendem Salz-
wasser blanchieren
und sofort abschrecken.
Die Korianderstängel
fein schneiden. Alle Zutaten zusammen vermengen
und mit der Gewürz-
mischung nach persönli-
chem Geschmack würzen.

GRÜNE BOHNEN
Bohnen dritteln, blanchieren und sofort abschre-
cken. — Die Zwiebel und die
Tomate in Würfel schnei-
den, den Knoblauch ha-
cken. — Etwas Öl in einer
Pfanne erhitzen und die
Zwiebeln darin anbraten.
Nach 4 Minuten den Knob-
lauch und den Kreuzküm-
mel hinzufügen und für
1 Minute mitdünsten. Dann
die blanchierten Bohnen
in die Pfanne geben und
auf hoher Flamme für 2–3
Minuten scharf anbraten.
Danach die gewürfel-
ten Tomaten, Tomaten-
mark und den Gemüse-
fond hinzugeben und auf
mittlerer Hitze für 10 Minuten köcheln lassen.
Mit Salz und einer Messer-
spitze Zimt abschmecken.

KORIANDER-
KARTOFFELN
Die Kartoffeln schälen,
in kleine Würfel schnei-
den und für 10 Minuten
in gesalzenem Wasser
kochen. Etwas Öl in eine
Pfanne geben und die
Koriandersamen sowie
den Knoblauch kurz
darin andünsten, bis die
Samen und der Kno-
blauch goldbraun sind.
— In einer weiteren
Pfanne Öl erhitzen und
die vorgekochten Kartof-
feln für 10 Minuten
scharf anbraten. Danach
den Knoblauch-Koriander-
Mix hinzufügen, gut ver-
mengen und mit frischem
Koriander garnieren.

ZUM ANRICHTEN
Das Taubenfleisch mit den
Fladenbrotbröseln be-
streuen und gemeinsam
mit den Beilagen auf
einem Teller anrichten.

ORIENTAL PIGEON WITH SIDE DISH VARIATIONS

SPICED OIL

Heat the olive, lemon, sesame and argan oil and add the spices. Fill a jar with the oil and leave to soak for approx. 1 week (this can be kept for 2 weeks if the jar is well closed and stored in a cool and dark place).

LENTIL SPICE MIX

Mix all ingredients together and set aside.

FLAT BREAD CRUMBS

Cut off the crusts and slice the bread into stripes. — Drizzle some oil onto it and bake for 15 minutes at 150°C until golden brown — Use a meat hammer and beat. Season the bread crumbs with some oil, pistachio semolina and lentil spice mix. Store in dry place.

PIGEON

Remove the pigeons breasts from the carcass and re-move the skin. Vacuum each breast with 10 ml of the spiced oil. — Cook the bags with the dove breasts for 8 minutes at 64.8°C in a water bath. Store the meat for about 20 minutes in heating cabinet. Once done, take the pigeon breasts out of the bags and drain the oil. Heat some clarified butter in a pan, add the herbs and the garlic and fry the breasts on both sides. Remove from the pan and allow to degrease on a paper towel. Season with salt and pepper.

Tip: The piece of meat can usually be vacuumed at the butcher's. On request, they certainly add a few brought herbs and spices!

LENTILS

Soak the lentils separately a day before. Coarsely cut the shallot and one half of the red pepper and sauté in sesame oil. Add the vegetable broth, bring to the boil and allow to cool down — Strain the lentils and cook (individually) in salted vegetable stock: cook the yellow and red lentils for 2 minutes and the remainder for 6–8 minutes. — Cut the second half of the pepper into small brunoise, blanch in salted water and immediately rinse with cold water. — Cut the coriander stems. Mix all ingredients and season with the lentil spice mix according to your taste.

GREEN BEANS

Cut the beans into mouth-sized pieces and blanch. — Cut the onion and tomato into pieces and finely slice the garlic. — Heat some oil in a pan and fry the onion. After approx. 4 minutes, add the garlic and cumin and steam for 1 minute. Add the beans and sear on high for 2–3 minutes. Afterwards, add the tomato pieces, tomato paste and vegetable stock and let simmer on medium for 10 minutes. Season with salt and a pinch of cinnamon.

CORIANDER-POTAOES

Peel the potatoes, cut into mouth-sized pieced and cook for 10 minutes in salted water. Heat some olive oil in a pan, add the finely chopped garlic and the coriander seeds and roast until golden brown. Set aside. In another pan, fry the precooked potatoes on high for 10 minutes. Add the garlic-coriander mix and serve with fresh coriander.

FOR SERVING

Sprinkle the pigeon with the pita bread crumbs and serve together with the side dishes.

AYRANSORBET AN DATTELCREME
AYRANSORBET WITH DATE CREAM

AYRANSORBET
Alle Zutaten vermengen und in einer Eismaschine gefrieren lassen. Direkt anrichten.

DATTELCREME
Die Datteln kleinschneiden und mit Orangensaft, Zitronenschale und Vanille aufkochen und abgedeckt über Nacht durchziehen lassen. Dann im Thermomix fein mixen und durch ein Spitzsieb passieren. Zum Schluss mit Blutorangensaft und Zitronensaft abschmecken.

KICHERERBSENPÜREE
Die Kichererbsen mit Cumin in Butter anschwitzen und mit Pernod ablöschen. Das Ganze reduzieren, bis der Pernod verdunstet, ist und mit Orangensaft auffüllen, bis die Kichererbsen gut bedeckt sind. Zimtstange, Zucker und Zitronenschale dazugeben und die Kichererbsen weich kochen. Anschließend mixen. Mit Orangensaft und Zucker abschmecken und durch ein Tuchsieb passieren.

ZUM ANRICHTEN
Eine Ayransorbet-Nocke formen und gemeinsam mit etwas Dattelcreme und Kichererbsenpüree servieren. Mit einzelnen Kichererbsen und einer Dattel dekorieren.

AYRAN SORBET
Mix all ingredients and freeze in an ice cream maker. Serve directly.

DATE CREAM
Finely chop the dates and bring to the boil with orange juice, lemon zest and vanilla pulp. Let it soak overnight with the lid closed. Finely mix in a thermomix and strain through a sieve. Season with red orange juice and lemon juice.

CHICKPEA MOUSSE
Sauté the chickpeas with cumin in butter and deglaze with Pernod. Reduce until the Pernod is evaporated and add orange juice, until the chickpeas are covered. Add the cinnamon stick, sugar and lemon zest and heat until the chickpeas are cooked through. Mix it with a blender and season with orange juice and sugar. Strain through a fine sieve.

FOR SERVING
Serve the Ayran sorbet together with some dates cream and chickpea mousse. Garnish with chickpeas and a date.

10

SOUL FOOD: VON AFFENBROTBÄUMEN UND KARTOFFELPUFFERN

SOUL FOOD: ON BAOBAB TREES AND POTATO CAKES

MOUHAMED & MATHIAS

Zwei Köche und Freunde, Mouhamed aus Niger und Mathias aus dem Allgäu, haben im Kitchen Hub zueinandergefunden. Beide sind über die Köchinnen ihrer Familie zum Kochen gekommen. Der eine hat eine Mutter, die alle 13 Kinder und die ganze Familie bekochte; der andere verbindet seine Lieblingsrezepte wie Maultaschen und Strudel mit seiner Großmutter. Die Sorgfalt und Geduld in der Zubereitung sowie die Ruhe, mit der eine Mahlzeit im Kreis der Familie eingenommen wird, machen für Mouhamed und Mathias den besonderen Reiz des Kochens aus. Gerichte, die so besonders nahrhaft werden, auch im übertragenen Sinne: echtes soul food eben. Kartoffelpuffer können da in Deutschland als Lieblingsspeise von Mouhamed mithalten. Für ihn darf es beim Kochen gerne schärfer zugehen und das Kuka-Gewürz aus den jungen Blättern der Affenbrotbäume tut sein Übriges für ein rundes Geschmackserlebnis.

Mouhamed erzählt, dass er das in Deutschland sehr verbreitete Essen in Restaurants nicht nachvollziehen kann. Dabei geht das gemeinsame Kochen verloren, die Begegnung, der Austausch, das Gespräch, alles, was Kochen auch bedeuten kann. Im Kreis von Mouhameds Familie werden auch die Verstorbenen einbezogen: Nach jeder Mahlzeit werfen die Familienmitglieder einen Happen auf den Boden, um so den Geist des verstorbenen Großvaters zu ehren. Wir sind alle mit unserer Familie und Herkunft verwurzelt und wie kann man das schöner feiern, als mit einem gemeinsam zubereiteten Gericht?

Two chefs and friends – Mouhamed from Niger and Mathias from the Allgäu region in southern Germany – have come together in the Kitchen Hub. Both found their way into cooking through the female cooks in their family: one of them by having a mother who cooked for all 13 of her children and the entire family, while the other is reminded of his grandmother by his favorite recipes such as Swabian ravioli and strudel. The care and patience in preparing food together coupled with the peacefulness in having a meal as a family, is what drew Mouhamed and Mathias to the art of cooking. In this way, meals become especially nutritious in both, the literal and figurative sense: true soul food as it were. In this respect, German potato pancakes can keep up as Mouhamed's favorite meal in Germany. For him, cooking is usually a spicy affair, with the Kuka-spice from the young leaves of the Baobab tree making for a full-flavored experience. Mouhamed tells us that he cannot relate to the concept of eating out in restaurants, which is so widespread in Germany. For him, the communal aspect of cooking is entirely lost: the encounter, exchange, and conversation – all the things that cooking also stands for. In Mouhamed's family, even the dead take part in the shared cooking experience: After every meal the family members throw a morsel of food on the ground to honor their late grandfather. We are all rooted in our families and our origins – and what way to better celebrate them than by preparing a meal together?

MENÜ

VORSPEISE

KNUSPRIGE HIRSEPUFFER MIT FEURIG- FRISCHEN DIPS

HAUPTSPEISE

WELSFILET IN KRÄUTERKRUSTE MIT DAN'WAKE

NACHSPEISE

ZART SCHMELZENDE SCHOKO- KÜCHLEIN AN MANGO-TAPIOKA

KNUSPRIGE HIRSE- PUFFER MIT FEURIG- FRISCHEN DIPS
Für die Hirsepuffer:
2 rote Bete
200 g Hirse
400 ml Gemüsebrühe
1 Ei
2 Eigelb
1 TL Orangenzeste
Sonnenblumenöl
frischer Majoran
Salz
Pfeffer

Für die Bananenchips:
2 Kochbananen
Pflanzenöl

Für den Tomaten-Dip:
2 große Tomaten
1 Chili (Habanero)
1 Zwiebel
2–3 EL Olivenöl
Salz
Pfeffer

Für das Erbsenpüree:
250 g gefrorene Erbsen
2 Knoblauchzehen
5 Stängel frische Minze

WELSFILET IN KRÄUTERKRUSTE MIT DAN'WAKE
Für den Fisch:
600 g Welsfilet
2 Schalotten
1 Brötchen vom Vortag
100 g Butter

4 EL frische Kräuter
der Saison
2 Eigelbe
2 Zitronen
etwas Weißwein
Olivenöl

Für die Zitronen- Rotkohl-Sauce:
2 Zwiebeln
500 gr Rotkohl
400 ml Gemüsebrühe
1 Karotte
1 Zitrone
ggf. etwas Speisestärke
zum Binden

Für das Dan'Wake:
200 g Bohnenmehl
300 ml warmes Wasser
2 EL Kuka-Pulver
(Baobab-Blätter)

ZART SCHMELZENDE SCHOKOKÜCHLEIN AN MANGO-TAPIOKA
Für die Küchlein:
200 g Zartbitterschokolade
80 g Butter
4 EL Mehl
2 Eier
60 g Zucker
30 g weiße Schokolade

Für das Mango-Tapioka:
1 Mango
100 g Perltapioka
450 ml Wasser
150 ml gezuckerte
Kondensmilch

CRISPY MILLET
FRITTERS WITH SPICY
AND FRESH DIPS

For the millet fritters:
2 red beets
200 g millet
400 ml vegetable stock
1 whole egg
2 egg yolks
1 tsp. orange zest
fresh marjoram
sunflower oil
salt
pepper

For the plantain chips:
2 plantains
vegetable oil

For the tomato dip:
2 large tomatoes
1 habanero chili
1 onion
2–3 Tbsp. olive oil
salt
pepper

For the pea puree:
250 g frozen peas
2 garlic cloves
5 sprigs of fresh mint

CATFISH FILLET
IN A HERBAL CRUST
WITH DAN'WAKE

For the fish:
600 g catfish fillet
2 shallots
1 piece of day-old bread
100 g butter

4 Tbsp. of fresh seasonal
herbs
2 egg yolks
2 lemons
white wine
olive oil

*For the red cabbage
and lemon sauce:*
2 onions
500 g red cabbage
400 ml vegetable stock
1 carrot
1 lemon
cornstarch

For the Dan'wake:
200 g bean flower
300 ml warm water
25 g Kuka powder
(Baobab leaves)

SOFTLY MELTING
CHOCOLATE
CAKES AND MANGO-
TAPIOCA

For the cakes:
200 g dark chocolate
80 g butter
4 Tbsp. flour
2 eggs
60 g sugar
30 g white chocolate

For the mango-tapioca:
1 mango
100 g tapioca pearls
450 ml water
150 ml sweetened
condensed milk

MENUE
SERVES 4

———————

STARTER

CRISPY MILLET
FRITTERS
WITH SPICY AND
FRESH DIPS

MAIN DISH

CATFISH FILLET
IN A HERBAL CRUST
WITH DAN'WAKE

DESSERT

SOFTLY MELTING
CHOCOLATE
CAKES AND
MANGO-TAPIOCA

KNUSPRIGE HIRSEPUFFER MIT FEURIG-FRISCHEN DIPS
CRISPY MILLET FRITTERS WITH SPICY AND FRESH DIPS

HIRSEPUFFER

Die Gemüsebrühe aufkochen. Die Hirse unter ständigem Rühren einrieseln lassen. — Bei geringer Hitze so lange köcheln lassen, bis die Hirse gar ist. — Die rote Bete schälen und grob reiben. Mit lauwarmer Hirse, einem ganzen Ei und 2 Eigelben sowie der Orangenzeste vermischen und mit Salz, Pfeffer und Majoran abschmecken. — Mit dem Esslöffel oder einem Portionierer zu kleinen Küchlein formen und in Sonnenblumenöl anbraten.

BANANENCHIPS

Die Kochbananen in gleich große Scheiben schneiden. — In sehr heißem Öl so lange backen, bis es keine Bläschen mehr am Rand der Scheiben gibt.

TOMATEN-DIP

Die Tomaten für ca. 2 Minuten in heißem Wasser kochen, bis sich die Haut löst. Danach mit kaltem Wasser abschrecken und schälen. — Die Zwiebeln hacken und die Chili fein schneiden. Alle Zutaten in einem Mixer zu einer cremigen Masse vermengen, danach mit Salz, Pfeffer und etwas Olivenöl abschmecken.

ERBSENPÜREE

Die Erbsen in kochendes Wasser geben und kurz blanchieren. — Die geschälten Knoblauchzehen im Mörser zerreiben und danach die Erbsen hinzugeben. — Alles langsam zermahlen und am Ende mit frisch gehackter Minze verfeinern.

MILLET FRITTERS

Bring the vegetable stock to the boil. Sprinkle in the millet and simmer on low heat, stirring continously until millet is cooked through. — Peel the red beets and grate coarsely. Add grated red beets, one whole egg plus the egg yolks and the orange zest to the lukewarm millet. — Season with salt, pepper and marjoram. — Shape the mixture into small cakes using a tablespoon or scoop and fry them in sunflower oil until golden brown.

PLANTAIN CHIPS

Peel and cut plantains into approx. 1 cm thick slices. — Deep-fry in very hot oil until no more bubbles appear at the edge of the slices.

TOMATO DIP

Cook whole tomatoes for 2 minutes in boiling water until the tomato peel comes off easily. Pour ice water over the tomatoes and peel them. — Finely chop onions and the chili. Mix all ingredients together in a blender and season with salt, pepper and a little olive oil.

PEA PUREE

Bring water to the boil and briefly blanch the peas. — Grind peeled garlic cloves in a mortar and pestle. — Add peas to the mortar and grind everything together slowly. Sprinkle with freshly chopped mint on top.

WELSFILET IN KRÄUTERKRUSTE MIT DAN'WAKE
CATFISH FILLET IN A HERBAL CRUST WITH DAN'WAKE

FISCH

Die Schalotten hacken und mit etwas Öl anbraten. Das Brötchen in Würfel schneiden und kurz mitbraten. Die Butter hinzugeben und alles gut vermischen. Dann die Kräuter fein hacken, hinzugeben und alles in eine extra Schale geben. — Nun die Eigelbe darunter mischen und den Mix auf dem Fischfilet verteilen. — Die Zitronen in feine Scheiben schneiden und in eine Auflaufform geben. — Etwas Butter in einer Pfanne schmelzen, mit Weißwein abgießen, in eine Auflaufform geben, das Welsfilet darauflegen und für ca. 12–15 Minuten im Ofen bei 160°C backen.

ZITRONEN-ROT-KOHLSAUCE

Die Zwiebeln würfeln und anbraten. — Den Rotkohl in sehr feine Streifen schneiden und die Karotte fein raspeln. Beides kurz mit anbraten, mit Gemüsebrühe ablöschen und etwa 10 Minuten köcheln lassen. — Die Zitrone auspressen und kurz vor Ende den Saft und je nach Geschmack etwas Zitronenzeste hinzugeben und für 1 Minute mitkochen. — Im Anschluss kräftig mixen und durch ein Sieb streichen. — Bei Bedarf noch mit Speisestärke abbinden.

DAN'WAKE

Das Bohnenmehl in eine große Schüssel geben und mit dem Kuka-Pulver vermischen. — Nun das Wasser hinzugeben und kräftig zu einem dehnbaren Teig kneten. — Einen großen Topf Salzwasser zum Kochen bringen. — Den Teig mit 2–3 Fingern in kleinere Portionen formen und in kochendem Wasser für ca. 10 Minuten kochen. Sofort servieren.

FISH

Chop the shallots and fry them in a pan with olive oil. Cube the bread and fry together with the shallots. — Add butter and mix well. — Chop the seasonal herbs, add them to he mixture and place everything together in a separate bowl. Mix in the egg yolks and spread the breading mixture on top of the catfish filet. — Cut lemons into fine slices and place them in a baking dish. — Melt some butter in a pan, deglaze with your favorite white wine and pour the mixture over the lemons in the baking dish. — Place catfish fillet with herbal crust on top and bake in the oven at 160°C for 12–15 minutes.

RED CABBAGE AND LEMON SAUCE

Dice and sauté the onions. — Cut the cabbage into fine strips and finely grate the carrot. Briefly sauté the vegetable mixture together with the onions. Pour the vegetable stock over the onions, cabbage and carrot, and let simmer for about 10 minutes. — Juice the lemon and add shortly before the end of the cooking process. Add some lemon zest according to taste. — Blend cooked vegetables and press through a sieve. If the sauce seems too thin, add a small amount of cornstarch to thicken.

DAN'WAKE

Mix together the bean flower and Kuka powder in a big bowl. Slowly add the water and mix into a flexible dough. Meanwhile, in a big pot, bring salted water to the boil. — Using 2–3 fingers, form small balls from the dough and cook them for about 10 minutes in boiling water. Serve immediately.

ZART SCHMELZENDE SCHOKOKÜCHLEIN AN MANGO-TAPIOKA
SOFTLY MELTING CHOCOLATE CAKES AND MANGO-TAPIOCA

KÜCHLEIN
Die dunkle Schokolade grob hacken und mit Butter in einem Wasserbad schmelzen. — Mehl, Eier und Zucker vermengen und die flüssige Schokolade unterrühren. — Die weiße Schokolade in 6 Stücke schneiden. — Den Teig in eingefetete Muffinförmchen füllen und jeweils ein Stück weiße Schokolade in den Teig drücken. — Die Küchlein im vorgeheizten Ofen bei 160°C Umluft für 25 Minuten backen.

MANGO-TAPIOKA
Das Wasser in einem Topf zum Kochen bringen. — Perltapioka hinzugeben und bei mittlerer Hitze ca. 3–4 Minuten quellen lassen. Dabei immer wieder umrühren. — Die Kondensmilch hinzugeben und 15 Minuten lang zu Ende garen, dabei häufig rühren. — Tapioka-Mix im Kühlschrank abkühlen lassen. — Die Mango schälen und das Fruchtfleisch mit etwa 2 EL Wasser pürieren. — Den Tapioka-Mix mit dem Mangomousse vermischen und zusammen mit den Schokoküchlein servieren.

CAKES
Coarsely chop the dark chocolate and melt together with the butter in a double boiler. — Mix together flour, eggs and sugar, and stir in the melted chocolate. — Cut the white chocolate into 6 pieces. — Pour the dough in a greased muffin pan. Drop a piece of white chocolate in each cake and allow to sink in completely. Bake in the oven for 25 minutes at 160°C.

MANGO-TAPIOCA
In a pot bring water to the boil. — Add tapioca pearls and allow to swell at medium heat for 3–4 minutes, stirring frequently. — Add sweetened condensed milk and cook for another 15 minutes, stirring continously. — Allow the tapioca mix to cool down in the fridge. — Meanwhile, peel the mango, and puree the fruit pulp together with 2 Tbsp. water. — Mix tapioca together with mango puree and serve with the chocolate cakes.

11

ALEPPOS KIRSCHEN
ALEPPO'S CHERRIES

MALLAKE & MICHA

In der Gegend rund um Aleppo gibt es ca. 300 verschiedene Kirschsorten. Eine Vielfalt, die Grundlage für ein typisches Gericht der regionalen syrischen Küche ist – Fleischbällchen an Kirschsauce. Die vielen Kirschen, die dafür benötigt werden, machen das Gericht teuer und so wird es zu besonderen Anlässen und für Familienfeierlichkeiten zubereitet, erzählt Mallake. Die junge Syrerin aus Damaskus ist Profiköchin und hat im syrischen Fernsehen gekocht. Sie beherrscht ihre Kunst, ebenso wie Micha Schäfer, der in Deutschland für einen radikal regionalen Ansatz steht – in seiner Küche wird ausschließlich und strikt regional gekocht. Er nennt das „brutal lokal". Das schließt auch Pfeffer und andere Gewürze aus. So weit wollte Mallake nicht gehen, denn ohne Zimt, Muskat und Nelken sei schwerlich ein syrisches Gericht zuzubereiten. Von dieser Ausnahme abgesehen nimmt Mallake die Herausforderung einer regional inspirierten Küche jedoch fröhlich und schwungvoll an: Die typische Nachspeise Mamounia, ein Grießpudding, wird hier mit Apfelkraut und Mozzarella abgewandelt. Eine sehr überzeugende Variante! Bald wird ihr eigenes Kochbuch mit Rezepten der syrischen Küche entstehen. Ihr Mann muss schon jetzt alles testen, was Mallake ausprobiert. Ob man da wirklich Mitleid haben muss? Eher nicht.

In the region of Aleppo, there are about 300 different kinds of cherries. A variety which led to the creation of a typical dish of Syrian regional cuisine - meatballs in cherry sauce. Because of the many cherries needed for its preparation, the dish is very expensive. This is why it is only served on special occasions and family events, explains Mallake. The young Syrian woman from Damascus is a professional chef and used to cook on Syrian TV. She is a master of her art just like Micha Schäfer, who is known in Germany for his strictly regional approach – his cooking style is defined by exclusively regional products. This even excludes pepper and other spices. Mallake, however, didn't want to go quite so far, because without cinnamon, nutmeg and cloves it is admittedly difficult to prepare any Syrian dish. But apart from this one exception, Mallake is excited and happy to take on the challenge of a regionally inspired cuisine: the typical dessert Mamounia, a semolina pudding, is now modified with applesyrup and mozzarella. A very convincing variation! Soon her own Syrian cookbook will be published. Until then, her husband already has to try all the things she's experimenting in the kitchen. Should we feel sorry for him? Probably not.

MENÜ

FÜR 4 PERSONEN

VORSPEISE

RAFFINIERTE FLEISCHBÄLLCHEN AN KIRSCHSAUCE

HAUPTSPEISE

GEFÜLLTE ZUCCHINI-TÜRMCHEN MIT LABNEH

NACHSPEISE

SÜßER GRIEß MIT HERZHAFTEM MOZZARELLA

RAFFINIERTE FLEISCHBÄLLCHEN AN KIRSCHSAUCE

Für die Fleischbällchen:
400 g Hackfleisch
(Rind oder Lamm)
50 g Petersilie
1 *Prise* Muskatnuss
1 *Prise* Zimt
1/4 *TL* Nelkenpulver
Pfeffer
Meersalz
1 *Handvoll* ganze Haselnüsse
Pflanzenöl

Für die Kirschsauce:
300 g entkernte Kirschen
150 ml Kirschsaft
2 *EL* Zucker
2 *EL* Zitronensaft

Zum Anrichten:
4 *Scheiben* Vollkornbrot
40 g Butter
3 *EL* Petersilie

GEFÜLLTE ZUCCHINI-TÜRMCHEN MIT LABNEH

Für den Labneh:
1 kg Joghurt, 10% Fett
1 *TL* Salz

Für die gefüllten Zucchini-Türmchen:
12 *kleine* Zucchini
8 Stangen Spargel
300 g Hackfleisch
(Rind oder Lamm)
8 Tomaten
60 g Tomatenmark
3 Knoblauchzehen
2 *TL* arabisches Siebengewürz
Salz
Pfeffer
etwas Butter zum Anbraten
100 ml Hühnerfond
Pflanzenöl

SÜßER GRIEß MIT HERZHAFTEM MOZZARELLA

Für das Apfelkraut:
5 kg reife Boskop-Äpfel
5 kg reife Elstar-Äpfel

Für den Grieß:
2 *EL* Ghee oder Butterschmalz
100 g grober Hartweizengrieß
500 ml Wasser
150 g Zucker
1 *Pkg.* Mozzarella
1 *TL* Zimt

MALLAKE & MICHA

FANCY MEATBALLS IN CHERRY SAUCE

For the meatballs:
400 g minced meat
(beef or lamb)
50 g parsley
1 pinch nutmeg
1 pinch cinnamon
1/4 tsp. ground cloves
pepper
sea salt
1 handful of whole hazelnuts
vegetable oil for frying

For the cherry sauce:
300 g cherries, pitted
150 ml cherry juice
2 Tbsp. sugar
2 Tbsp. lemon juice

For serving:
4 slices wholemeal bread
butter
3 Tbsp. parsley

STUFFED ZUCCHINI TOWERS WITH LABNEH

For the labneh:
500 g yoghurt, 10% fat
1/2 tsp. salt

For the stuffed zucchini towers:
12 small zucchini
8 asparagus spears
300 g minced meat
(beef or lamb)
8 tomatoes
60 g of tomato paste
3 garlic cloves
2 tsp. Arabic 7-spice
salt
pepper
some butter for frying
100 ml chicken stock
vegetable oil

SWEET SEMOLINA PORRIDGE WITH MOZZARELLA

For the apple syrup:
5 kg ripe "Belle de Boskoop"
apples
5 kg ripe Elstar apples

For the semolina porridge:
2 Tbsp. ghee or clarified butter
100 g coarse semolina
500 ml water
150 g sugar
1 pack mozzarella
1 tsp. cinnamon

MENUE

SERVES 4

───────────

STARTER

FANCY MEATBALLS IN CHERRY SAUCE

MAIN DISH

STUFFED ZUCCHINI TOWERS WITH LABNEH

DESSERT

SWEET SEMOLINA PORRIDGE WITH MOZZARELLA

RAFFINIERTE FLEISCHBÄLLCHEN AN KIRSCHSAUCE

FANCY MEATBALLS IN CHERRY SAUCE

FLEISCHBÄLLCHEN

Die Petersilie fein hacken. Muskat, Zimt, Nelken- pulver und die gehackte Petersilie zum Hackfleisch hinzugeben und gut vermengen. Mit Salz und Pfeffer abschmecken. Aus dem gewürzten Hack- fleisch kleine Bällchen formen und in jedes Bäll- chen eine ganze Hasel- nuss stecken und wieder verschließen. In einer Pfanne Pflanzenöl erhitzen und die Bällchen bei ho- her Hitze scharf anbraten und zur Seite legen.

KIRSCHSAUCE

Die Kirschen zusammen mit dem Kirschsaft pü- rieren und dann durch ein feines Sieb passieren.

Den Kirschsaft aufkochen, 2 EL Zucker hinzugeben und mit 2 EL Zitronensaft einkochen lassen, bis eine sirupähnliche Konsistenz entstanden ist. Die Bällchen für 3 Minuten zum Fertig- garen in die Sauce legen.

ZUM ANRICHTEN

Petersilie fein hacken. But- ter schmelzen und kurz vor dem Anrichten das Brot darin wenden, auf Back- papier legen, mit Meersalz bestreuen und für 3 Minuten im vorgeheizten Backofen bei 180°C knusprig backen. Zum Servieren je 3–4 Bällchen auf eine Brot- scheibe legen, die Kirsch- sauce darüber geben und mit etwas frischer Petersilie dekorieren.

MEATBALLS

Finely chop the parsley and add to the minced meat along with the nutmeg, cinnamon and ground cloves. Mix well and season with salt and pepper. Form small balls out of the meat. Put one hazelnut in each ball and reseal. — Heat vegetable oil in a pan and fry the balls on high heat until cooked through and set aside.

CHERRY SAUCE

Blend cherries together with cherry juice and pass through a fine sieve. Bring cherry juice to the boil, add the sugar and the lemon juice. Cook until a jelly-like con- sistency is obtained. Place the meatballs in the cherry sauce and cook for 3 minutes or until cooked through.

FOR SERVING

Finely chop the parsley. Melt some butter and coat the bread in it just before ser- ving. Place on a baking sheet, sprinkle with sea salt and bake in the preheated oven at 180°C for 3 minutes until crispy. For serving, place 3–4 meatballs on each slice of bread, sprinkle the cherry sauce over it and garnish with the freshly chopped parsley.

GEFÜLLTE ZUCCHINI-TÜRMCHEN MIT LABNEH
STUFFED ZUCCHINI TOWERS WITH LABNEH

LABNEH

Ein großes Sieb mit mehreren Lagen Käseleinen oder mit einem Mulltuch auslegen. Joghurt mit dem Salz verrühren und ins Sieb geben. Sieb auf eine große Schüssel setzen, damit die Molke ablaufen kann und 24 Stunden abtropfen lassen. Falls die Masse noch zu flüssig ist, am nächsten Morgen mit den Händen nochmal leicht ausdrücken. Je länger dem Joghurt so die Molke entzogen wird, desto fester wird der Frischkäse.

ZUCCHINI-TÜRMCHEN

Zucchini und Spargel in ca. 4 cm lange Stücke schneiden. Dann die Zucchini so aushöhlen, dass auf einer Seite ein Boden vorhanden bleibt. — Nun das Hackfleisch in etwas Butter anbraten. Nach ca. 3 Minuten Salz und Pfeffer dazugeben. — Die Tomaten fein würfeln und mit dem Tomatenmark, gehacktem Knoblauch und dem Arabischen Siebengewürz in einem kleinen Topf zu einer Tomatensauce kochen. Nach einigen Minuten mit etwas Hühnerfond auffüllen und weiter reduzieren, mit Salz und Pfeffer abschmecken. — Die Zucchini mit dem Hackfleisch befüllen. Öl in einer Pfanne erhitzen, die gefüllten Zucchini-Türmchen aufrecht in das Öl stellen und für einige Minuten darin frittieren. — Im Anschluss die Zucchini-Türmchen in eine Auflaufform geben und die Spargelstücke dazwischen stellen. Jetzt die Tomatensauce dazugeben. Idealerweise sind Spargel und Zucchini-Türmchen zur Hälfte von der Sauce bedeckt. Für 15 Minuten bei 180°C im Ofen schmoren. — Die frisch gebackenen Zucchini-Türmchen und Spargelstangen zusammen mit der Tomatensauce auf einem Teller anrichten und dazu den frischen Labneh servieren.

LABNEH

Line a large sieve with several layers of cheesecloth. Mix yoghurt and salt and pour the mix into the sieve. Place the sieve on a large bowl and allow to drain for 24 hours. If the mass is still too liquid the next morning, squeeze the liquid out of the mass using your fingers. The longer the whey is removed, the firmer the cheese becomes.

ZUCCHINI TOWERS

Cut the zucchini and asparagus in 4 cm long pieces. Then scoop out the zucchini so that one base is left in each piece. — In a pan, fry the minced meat with some butter. After about 3 minutes, season with salt and pepper. — Dice tomatoes and cook together with tomato paste, garlic and the Arabic 7-spice until it is cooked down to a tomato sauce. After a few minutes, deglaze with chicken stock and cook for a few more minutes, then season with salt and pepper. — Fill the zucchini with the minced meat. Heat the oil in a pan and put the stuffed zucchini towers upright in the oil. Deep-fry for a few minutes. — Place the zucchini towers in a baking dish and put the asparagus pieces in between them. Pour the tomato sauce into the dish. The asparagus and the zucchini towers should be half-covered in sauce. Cook in the oven at 180°C for 15 minutes. — Serve together with fresh labneh.

SÜßER GRIEß MIT HERZHAFTEM MOZZARELLA
SWEET SEMOLINA WITH MOZZARELLA

APFELKRAUT
Die Äpfel entsaften und durch ein Tuch passieren. Den Saft aufkochen und so lange einreduzieren bis eine dickflüssige, säuerliche Masse entsteht. Dieser Vorgang dauert je nach Menge und Herd mehrere Stunden. Dann wird der Sirup in Einmachgläser gefüllt und kaltgestellt.

Tipp: Je nach Erntedatum der Äpfel variiert die Säure und Süße des Apfelkrauts.

GRIESS
Das Wasser und den Zucker zu einem Sirup einkochen, zur Seite stellen und ab-kühlen lassen. Ghee in einem Topf schmelzen und den Grieß hinzugeben. Den Grieß langsam und unter ständigem Rühren so lange rösten, bis er eine kräftige, aber nicht zu dunkelbraune Färbung bekommt. So entwickelt sich ein ganz spezielles, nussiges Aroma. Den Grieß langsam in den lauwarmen Sirup geben und kräftig umrühren. — Zum Anrichten den Grieß in einer Schale servieren und den Mozzarella in dünnen Scheiben darüber geben. Mit Zimt und Apfelkraut verfeinern und bei Bedarf ein wenig geschmolzenes Ghee hinübergeben.

APPLE SYRUP
Juice the apples and pass through a cloth. Bring juice to the boil and cook until a thick and sourish syrup is formed. This process may need hours depending on the amount and the type of stove.
— Pour syrup in preserving jars and keep cold.

Tip: The acidity and sweetness of the apple syrup varies greatly from the date of harvest.

SWEET SEMOLINA
Boil the sugar and water down to a syrup, set aside and allow to cool. Melt ghee in a saucepan and add the semolina. Roast semolina slowly, stirring constantly until it gets an intense (but not too dark) brown color. This will give the semolina a very special flavor. Carefully add the roasted semolina to the luke-warm syrup and stir thoroughly. — Serve the sweet semolina in a bowl and garnish with thin slices of mozzarella. For a final touch, sprinkle some cinnamon and apple syrup, and add some melted ghee according to taste.

FATIR FÜR ALLE
FATIR FOR EVERYONE

AHMED & HARALD

In jedem ägyptischen Dorf wird Fatir, eine Art Pfannkuchen, zubereitet; jeder Dörfler hat sein eigenes Rezept. Hier wird uns eine besonders fantasievolle Variante als Dessert aufgetischt. Zusammen mit dem gebürtigen Österreicher Harald kreiert Ahmed im Atelier Culinário einen Fatir-Pfannkuchen mit Limetteneis und Zwetschgenröster. Fatir par excellence, eine wundervoll süße Brücke zwischen Ägypten und Österreich. Das Dessert krönt zum Abschluss ein Menü aus Sternanis-Karotten mit einem Dip und confiertem Zander an traditionellem Linsensalat. In der Fusion Cuisine ist die ganze Welt ein Dorf. Fatir! Für alle!

Fatir, a kind of pancake, is prepared in every Egyptian village; and every villager has his very own recipe for it. Here a very imaginative variation is served for dessert. In the Atelier Culinário, Ahmed and the native-born Austrian Harald are creating a Fatir-pancake with lime ice cream and plum compote. Fatir par excellence, a wonderfully sweet bridge between Egypt and Austria. The dessert crowns a brilliant menu of star-anise-carrots with a dip as well as confit zander on a bed of traditional lentil salad. In fusion cuisine the entire world is one village. Fatir! For everyone!

MENÜ

VORSPEISE

STERNANIS-KAROTTEN MIT GRANATAPFEL-DIP

HAUPTSPEISE

CONFIERTER ZANDER AN SCHWARZEM LINSENSALAT

NACHSPEISE

FATIR MIT ZWETSCHGEN-RÖSTER UND LIMETTENEIS

STERNANIS-KAROTTEN

Für die Sternanis-Karotten:
4 Karotten
2 Anissterne
1 ganze Vanilleschote
60 g Rohrzucker
1 EL Honig
150 g Butter
150 ml Weißwein
600 ml Gemüsebrühe
2 EL Fischsauce
Salz

Für den Granatapfel-Dip:
250 g Joghurt, 10% Fett
2 EL Limettensaft
1 1/2 TL Kreuzkümmel
1/2 TL Ras el Hanout
1 TL Schwarzkümmel
1 EL Tahina
1 EL frische Granatapfelkerne
1 EL Saft vom Granatapfel
Salz

Zum Anrichten:
1 *Handvoll* frische Minze
1 *Handvoll* frischer Koriander
Olivenöl

ZANDER AN
SCHWARZEM
LINSENSALAT
Für das Zanderfilet:
800 g Zanderfilet
400 ml Olivenöl
2 Anissterne
1 EL Koriandersamen
1 Zimtstange
20 g Thymian

Für den Linsensalat:
250 g schwarze Linsen
500 ml Wasser
1 1/2 Paprika (rot, gelb, grün)
6 Kirschtomaten

1 Zitrone
1/2 Orange
2 EL Olivenöl
2 TL Kreuzkümmel
Salz

Zum Anrichten:
1 rote Paprika
1 Frühlingszwiebel
Olivenöl, Meersalz

FATIR MIT ZWETSCHGEN-
RÖSTER UND LIMETTENEIS
Für den Fatir-Teig:
1 kg Mehl
1 Prise Salz
1 Prise Zucker
550 ml lauwarmes Wasser
100 g Butter
Pflanzenöl
Puderzucker
Honig

Für den Zwetschgenröster:
200 g Zwetschgen
100 ml Rotwein
70 g Zucker
40 g Butter
2 EL Rum (38% Alk.)
1 Zimtstange
2 Nelken
1 Vanillestange
1 Zimtblüte
2 Pimentkörner
3 EL Speisestärke

Für das Sauerrahm-Limetteneis:
1 kg Sauerrahm
2 *Blätter* Gelatine
1 Orange
2 Limetten
300 g Zucker

Zum Anrichten:
Honig, Puderzucker

STAR-ANISE-CARROTS

For the star-anise-carrots:
4 carrots
2 star anise
1 vanilla pod
60 g cane sugar
1 Tbsp. honey
150 g butter
150 ml white wine
600 ml vegetable stock
2 Tbsp. fish sauce
salt

For the pomegranate dip:
250 g yoghurt, 10% fat
2 Tbsp. lime juice
1 1/2 tsp. cumin
1/2 tsp. ras el hanout
1 tsp. black cumin seeds
1 Tbsp. tahini
1 Tbsp. fresh pomegranate
seeds
1 Tbsp. pomegranate juice
salt

For serving:
1 handful fresh mint
1 handful fresh coriander
olive oil

ZANDER WITH BLACK LENTIL SALAD

For the confit zander:
800 g zander fillet
400 ml olive oil
2 star anise
1 Tbsp. coriander seeds
1 cinnamon stick
20 g thyme

For the black lentil salad:
250 g black lentils
500 ml water
1 1/2 bell pepper (rot, gelb, grün)

6 cherry tomatoes
1 lemon
1/2 orange
2 Tbsp. olive oil
2 tsp. cumin
salt

For serving:
1 red bell pepper
1 spring onion
olive oil, sea salt

FATIR WITH ROASTED PLUMS AND LIME ICE

For the fatir:
1 kg flour
1 pinch of salt
1 pinch of sugar
550 ml lukewarm water
100 g butter
vegetable oil

For the roasted plums:
200 g plums
100 ml red wine
70 g sugar
40 g butter
2 Tbsp. rum (38% alc.)
1 cinnamon stick
2 cloves
1 vanilla pod
1 cinnamon blossom
2 allspice corns
3 Tbsp. cornstarch

For the lime ice cream:
1 kg sour cream
2 gelatin leaves
1 orange
2 limes
300 g sugar

For serving:
honey, icing sugar

MENUE

SERVES 4

———————

STARTER

STAR-ANISE-CARROTS WITH POME-GRANATE DIP

MAIN DISH

CONFIT ZANDER WITH BLACK LENTIL SALAD

DESSERT

FATIR WITH ROASTED PLUMS AND LIME ICE CREAM

STERNANIS-KAROTTEN MIT GRANATAPFEL-DIP
STAR-ANISE-CARROTS WITH POMEGRANATE DIP

STERNANIS-KAROTTEN
Den Sternanis mahlen und die Vanilleschote der Länge nach aufschneiden und das Mark herauskratzen. — Den Rohrzucker in einer Pfanne karamellisieren und im Anschluss Honig, Sternanis, Vanillemark und die Butter hinzugeben und mit Weißwein ablöschen. — Weißwein auf die Hälfte einreduzieren und dann mit Brühe aufgießen. Fischsauce und Salz hinzugeben und wieder bis zur Hälfte einreduzieren. Die Karotten dazugeben und im Ofen bei 180°C für 30 Minuten schmoren.

Tipp: Der Sud kann eingefroren und ein weiteres Mal verwendet werden!

Tipp: Wenn man keinen Wein zur Hand hat, kann man auch einfach 100 ml mehr Gemüsebrühe verwenden.

ZUBEREITUNG DES GANATAPFEL-DIPS
Alle Zutaten vermengen und mit Salz abschmecken.

ZUM ANRICHTEN
Das Gericht schmeckt besonders gut mit einem kleinen Salat aus frischer Minze, frischem Koriander und etwas Olivenöl.

STAR-ANISE-CARROTS
Grind the star anise. Cut vanilla in half and scrape out the pulp. Caramelize cane sugar and then add honey, ground star anise and vanilla pulp. Add the butter and deglaze with white wine. — Boil the white wine down to half and then pour in the vegetable broth. Add the fish sauce and salt, and boil down again to half. Then add the carrots and cook all together in the oven at 180°C for 30 minutes.

Tip: You can freeze the stock and use it another time!

Tip: If no wine is ready to hand, you can easily use 100 ml more vegetable stock.

POMEGRANATE DIP
Mix all ingredients together and season with salt.

FOR SERVING
The dish tastes great with a mix of fresh mint and fresh coriander, sprinkled with olive oil.

CONFIERTER ZANDER AN SCHWARZEM LINSENSALAT
CONFIT ZANDER WITH BLACK LENTIL SALAD

ZANDER
Die Gewürze in Olivenöl im Ofen bei 50°C für 10 Minuten ziehen lassen. Den Zander im aromatischen Öl bei 56°C (Kerntemperatur) im Ofen für 20 Minuten confieren.

LINSENSALAT
Wasser in einem Topf zum Kochen bringen und die Linsen darin für ca. 30 Minuten kochen, bis sie gar sind. In der Zwischenzeit die Tomaten und die Paprika in kleine Würfel schneiden, die Zitrone und die Orange pressen und den Saft auffangen. Alle Zutaten miteinander vermengen und mit Salz, Kreuzkümmel und Olivenöl abschmecken.

ZUM ANRICHTEN
Die rote Paprika schälen und die Schale in dünne Streifen schneiden. Das Grüne der Frühlingszwiebel ebenfalls in sehr feine Streifen schneiden und im Anschluss beides in Eiswasser legen. Nach ca. 5 Stunden beginnen sich die Frühlingszwiebel wie auch die Paprikastreifen spiralförmig einzurollen. Zander und Linsensalat anrichten, mit gekräuselter Frühlingszwiebel und Paprika dekorieren und mit Olivenöl sowie grobem Meersalz verfeinern.

CONFIT ZANDER
Infuse the spices in olive oil for 10 minutes in the oven at 50°C. Once done, use the aromatic oil to confit the zander fillet in the oven at 56°C (internal temperature) for 20 minutes.

BLACK LENTIL SALAD
In a pot, bring water to the boil and cook the lentils for about 30 minutes until tender. In the meantime, cut tomatoes and bell peppers into small cubes, juice the lemon and 1/2 orange. Mix all ingredients together and season with salt, cumin, and olive oil.

FOR SERVING
Peel red pepper and cut the peel into thin strips. Cut the spring onion into very fine strips as well, and place both in ice water. After approx. 5 hours, the spring onions and the bell pepper peel start to form spiral curls. Place zander fillet and lentil salad on a plate, decorate with the curls, and season with olive oil and sea salt.

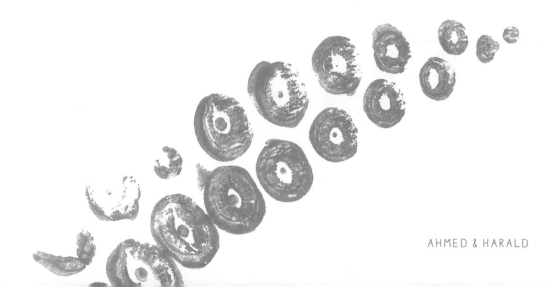

FATIR MIT ZWETSCHGENRÖSTER UND LIMETTENEIS
FATIR WITH ROASTED PLUMS AND LIME ICE

FATIR

Wasser, Mehl, Salz und Zucker zu einem Teig kneten und kleine Bälle formen. Fatir besteht aus 7 Schichten und somit werden 7 kleine Teigbällchen pro Fatir benötigt. Die Bälle mit reichlich Pflanzenöl bepinseln, zu Fladen ausrollen und jeden Fladen mit Frischhaltefolie abgedeckt für 20 Minuten ruhen lassen. — Die Butterschmelzen. Den Teig sehr dünn ausrollen und mit Butter bepinseln. Den Teig in die gewünschte Form falten und jede Lage erneut mit Butter bepinseln. — Auf einem eingefettetem Backblech bei 180°C jede Seite ca. 8 Minuten backen, bis der Teig goldbraun ist.

ZWETSCHGENRÖSTER

Zucker zusammen mit den Gewürzen karamellisieren, Butter hinzugeben und mit Rotwein ablöschen. Rum hinzugeben und auf 1/3 reduzieren. Danach mit Speisestärke binden, die frischen, entkernten Zwetschgen hinzugeben und für ca. 15 Minuten leicht köcheln lassen, bis die Zwetschgen weich sind, aber nicht zerkocht. Wenn nötig kann der Sud noch einmal mit Speisestärke leicht gebunden werden.

Tipp: Der Rotwein kann durch Zwetschgensaft ersetzt werden. Dabei sollte der Zuckeranteil um die Hälfte reduziert und ein wenig mehr Vanille verwendet werden.

LIMETTENEIS

Die 2 Blätter Gelatine in kaltem Wasser einweichen. Die Schale der Orange und der Limetten fein abreiben und die Früchte auspressen. Den Orangensaft zum Kochen bringen und bis zur Hälfte einreduzieren. Darin die eingeweichte Gelatine auflösen. — Den Sauerrahm mit dem Zucker und der fein geriebenen Orangen- und Limettenschale verrühren. Den Orangensaft mit der aufgelösten Gelatine zügig unterrühren und mit Limettensaft abschmecken. Die fertige Masse in eine Eismaschine geben und bis zur gewünschten Konsistenz warten.

ZUM ANRICHTEN

Fatir mit Puderzucker und Honig verfeinern und gemeinsam mit der frischen Eiscreme und dem noch leicht warmen Zwetschgnröster servieren.

FATIR

Knead water, flour, salt and sugar into a dough, then form 7 small balls out of the dough. Fatir traditionally consists of 7 layers and thus 7 small dough balls are needed. Brush the balls generously with vegetable oil, roll out into little pizzas, cover each pizza with cling film and allow to sit for 20 minutes. — Next, slowly melt the butter, roll out the dough very thinly and brush with melted butter. Fold the dough into the desired shape and brush each layer with melted butter.— Place layers on a greased baking tray and bake at 180°C for 8 minutes until golden.

ROASTED PLUMS

Caramelize sugar together with the spices, add butter and deglaze with red wine. Add rum and boil down to one third. Then bind with cornstarch, add the fresh, pitted plums and let simmer for about 15 minutes until plums are soft but not overcooked. If needed, bind the sauce again with cornstarch.

Tip: You can substitute the red wine with plum juice. However, the amount of sugar should be reduced by half and some more vanilla should be used.

LIME ICE CREAM

Allow gelatin to soak in cold water. Finely grate the peel of the orange and the lime, and juice the fruits separately. Bring the orange juice to the boil and boil down to half. Add the gelatin and allow it to dissolve while stirring. — Mix sour cream together with the sugar, finely grated orange and lime peel. Quickly stir in the orange juice with the dissolved gelatin and season with lime juice.— Put the mass into an ice cream maker and wait for desired consistency.

FOR SERVING

Refine the fatir with icing sugar and honey and serve together with a scoop of ice cream and a portion of roasted plums.

1 Aus dem Teig kleine Bälle formen und mit reichlich Öl bepinseln. Form small balls out of the dough and brush them generously with oil. 2 Die Bälle zu Fladen ausrollen. Roll out into small pizzas. 3 Die Fladen mit Frischhaltefolie bedeckt 20 Minuten ruhen lassen. Cover the pizzas with cling film and allow to rest for 20 minutes. 4 Die Fladen erneut dünn ausrollen und mit geschmolzener Butter bepinseln. Roll out the pizzas again very thinly and brush each with melted butter. 5 Den Teig in die gewünschte Form falten und jede Lage erneut mit Butter bepinseln. Fold the pizzas into the desired shape and brush each layer with melted butter. 6 Wiederholen, bis 7 Schichten aufeinander gelegt wurden. Repeat until all 7 layers are on top of each other.

13

MÄRKISCH-SYRISCHE HEIMATKÜCHE

A VERY OWN SYRIAN CUISINE FROM THE MARK OF BRANDENBURG

HADI

Hadi aus Aleppo verschlug es mit einigem Glück in unzähligen Stunden des mühsamen Reisens nach Berlin. Eine lange Reihe an Zufällen machte ihn vom einstigen Web Developer in Aleppo zum Koch in Berlin-Schöneberg: Er stolperte durch eine Bekannte ins Kitchen Hub, just als dringend ein Koch gesucht wurde, kochte und kochte wieder für uns von *Über den Tellerrand*. Ganz zufällig machte er ein Praktikum in der Küche des Neni im Bikini Haus in Berlin und landete schließlich als Koch im Restaurant Wolff & Eber, das er mit seiner regionalen, saisonalen und märkisch-syrischen Küche zu einer Heimat der Fusion-Cuisine gemacht hat. Alles rein zufällig natürlich. Na gut, sehr viel Können war schon auch im Spiel. Wir sind sehr glücklich über die positiven Wendungen in seinem Leben. Von seiner kulinarischen Meisterschaft haben wir oft profitiert, jetzt seid Ihr dran! Immer dem Rezept nach und schon landet man in der syrischen Mark Brandenburg. Oder im märkischen Syrien? Wie auch immer, man reist mit seinen Rezepten zu den Orten, die als die schönsten auf der Landkarte der Kulinarik vermerkt sind. Gute Reise!

With quite some luck over countless hours of arduous journeying, Hadi wound up in Berlin. A long series of coincidences made the former web Designer from Aleppo to a chef in Berlin-Schöneberg: a friend introduced him to the Kitchen Hub just as a chef was being urgently sought. After cooking for the first time, he cooked again and again for us at *Über den Tellerrand*. Afterwards, being a trainee at the Neni in the Bikini Haus in Berlin, he, by pure coincidence, finally ended up as a chef in the Restaurant Wolff & Eber. He made the place into a home of fusion cuisine with his regional, seasonal and märkisch-Syrian style. Everything by mere chance, of course. Fair enough, a huge amount of talent was also at play. We are proud and happy about the recent turns his life has taken for the better. Often enough, we benefited from his culinary skills, now it is your turn! Just follow the recipe and soon you will find yourself in the Syrian Mark of Brandenburg or, no, in märkisch Syria? Whatever it may be, with Hadi's recipes you will surely travel to the most beautiful places noted on the map for their culinary delights. Enjoy your trip!

194

MENÜ

VORSPEISE

KAYADI-SUPPE
MIT KOKOSNOTE

HAUPTSPEISE

HIRSCHGULASCH
MIT KABSA-
GEWÜRZREIS

NACHSPEISE

KNUSPRIGE
MAMUL-KEKSE
MIT PISTAZIEN

**KAYADI-SUPPE
MIT KOKOSNOTE**

Für die Suppe:
3 Kartoffeln
4 Karotten
2 Zwiebeln
250 g Sellerie
1 EL Pflanzenöl
200 ml Kokosnussmilch
1 EL Kurkuma
1 EL Curry
1 EL Tomatenmark
1 TL Salz
1 TL arabisches Siebengewürz
1 TL schwarzer Pfeffer
1 TL Paprikapuder
1 l Wasser

Zum Anrichten:
Arabisches Brot
Olivenöl
1 *Handvoll* Minzblätter

**HIRSCHGULASCH MIT
KAPSA-GEWÜRZREIS**

Für das Hirschfleisch:
500 g Hirschfleisch
150 g getrocknete Feigen
1 l Orangensaft
200 ml Rotwein
1 EL Kurkuma

1 EL Curry
1 TL Salz
1 TL Pfeffer
1 TL arabisches Siebengewürz
100 g Butter

Für den Kabsa-Gewürzreis:
250 g Basmatireis
150 g Cashewkerne
150 g Rosinen
50 g Butter
1 TL Salz
1 TL Pfeffer
1 TL arabisches Siebengewürz
1 TL Curry
Pflanzenöl zum Frittieren

**KNUSPRIGE
MAMUL-KEKSE
MIT PISTAZIEN**
500 g Mehl
500 g Grieß
350 g Butter
250 ml lauwarmes Wasser
100 g Puderzucker
150 g Pistazien
3 EL Rosenwasser

Zum Anrichten:
Puderzucker
2 EL geraspelte Pistazien

KAYADI SOUP WITH A SOFT HINT OF COCONUT

3 potatoes
4 carrots
2 onions
250 g celery
1 Tbsp. vegetable oil
250 ml coconut milk
1 Tbsp. curcuma
1 Tbsp. curry
1 Tbsp. tomato paste
1 tsp. salt
1 tsp. Arabic 7-spice
1 tsp. black pepper
1 tsp. paprika powder
1 l water

For Serving:
Arabic bread
olive oil
1 *handful* fresh mint

VENISON GOULASH WITH KABSA RICE

For the venison goulash:
500 g venison meat
150 g dried figs
1 l orange juice
200 ml red wine
1 Tbsp. curcuma
1 Tbsp. curry
1 tsp. salt
1 tsp. pepper
1 tsp. Arabic 7-spice
100 g butter

For the kabsa rice:
250 g basmati rice
150 g cashews
150 g raisins
50 g butter
1 tsp. salt
1 tsp. pepper
1 tsp. Arabic 7-spice
1 tsp. curry
vegetable oil

CRISPY MAMUL BISCUITS WITH PISTACHIOS

500 g flour
500 g semolina
350 g butter
250 ml water
100 g icing sugar
150 g pistachios
3 Tbsp. rose water

For serving:
icing sugar
2 Tbsp. pistachios, grated

MENUE

SERVES 4

———————

STARTER

KAYADI SOUP WITH A SOFT HINT OF COCONUT

MAIN DISH

VENISON GOULASH WITH KABSA RICE

Ⓥ

DESSERT

CRISPY MAMUL BISCUITS WITH PISTACHIOS

KAYADI-SUPPE MIT KOKOSNOTE
KAYADI SOUP WITH A SOFT HINT OF COCONUT

SUPPE
Das Gemüse in mundgerechte Stücke schneiden. Die Zwiebeln und den Sellerie in etwas Pflanzenöl anbraten, nach 4 Minuten das restliche Gemüse hinzufügen und kurz mitdünsten. Mit 1 l Wasser auffüllen und für weitere 10 Minuten köcheln lassen. Im Anschluss die Gewürze, das Tomatenmark und die Kokosnussmilch hinzugeben. Für weitere 15–20 Minuten kochen lassen, bis das Gemüse gar ist und im Anschluss pürieren.

ZUM ANRICHTEN
Das arabische Brot in Streifen schneiden und mit etwas Olivenöl beträufeln. Im Ofen bei 180°C für ca. 8 Minuten goldbraun werden lassen und zur Suppe reichen. Mit frischen Minzblättern dekorieren.

SOUP
Cut all vegetables into mouth-sized pieces. Heat some oil in a pan and sauté the onions together with the celery for 4 minutes. Afterwards, add all other vegetables and the water and bring it to the boil. Then add the spices, the tomato paste, and the coconut milk and let it boil for approx. 15–20 minutes. Mix everything with a blender.

FOR SERVING
Cut the Arabic bread into strips and sprinkle with olive oil. Bake in a preheated oven at 180°C for 8 minutes until golden and serve with the soup. Garnish with some fresh mint leaves.

HIRSCHGULASCH MIT KABSA-GEWÜRZREIS
VENISON GOULASH WITH KABSA RICE

HIRSCHFLEISCH

Das Hirschfleisch in Würfel schneiden und mit Orangensaft, Wein, den getrockneten Feigen, Kurkuma, Curry, Salz, Pfeffer und arabischem Siebengewürz für mindestens 12 Stunden im Kühlschrank marinieren. Das Fleisch zusammen mit der Marinade und der Butter in einer Ofenform bei 175°C für 45–55 Minuten garen.

KABSA-GEWÜRZREIS

Die Cashewkerne in etwas Butter rösten, bis sie goldbraun sind. Die Rosinen in Pflanzenöl frittieren und dann zur Seite stellen. Den Reis mit ca. 500 ml Wasser, Curry, Salz, schwarzem Pfeffer und arabischem Siebengewürz auf geringer Hitze garen lassen. Sobald der Reis gar ist, die Butter sowie die Nüsse und Rosinen hinzufügen und für 15 Minuten ruhen lassen. — Zum Anrichten das zarte Hirschfleisch mit dem Kabsa-Gewürzreis servieren und mit etwas zerlassener Butter beträufeln.

VENISON GOULASH

Cut the meat into cubes and marinate with orange juice, wine, figs, curcuma, curry, salt, black pepper and Arabic 7-spices. Leave it in the fridge for at least 12 hours. — Then cook the meat with the marinade and the butter in a big tray at 175°C for 45–55 minutes.

KABSA RICE

Roast the cashews in some butter until light brown and fry the raisins in vegetable oil. Set aside. Bring approx. 500 ml to the boil. Add the rice, curry, salt, black pepper, Arabic 7-spice and cook on medium until done. — As soon as the rice is done, add butter, the roasted chashew kernels and the raisins and let rest for approx. 15 minutes with the lid closed.

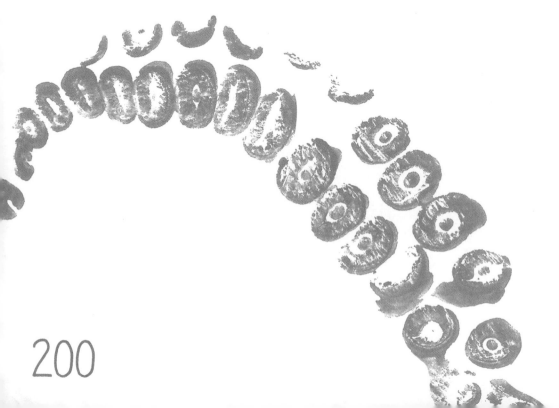

200

KNUSPRIGE MAMUL-KEKSE
MIT PISTAZIEN
CRISPY MAMUL BISCUITS
WITH PISTACHIOS

TEIG
Mehl, Grieß und Puderzu-
cker vermengen. Danach
250 g geschmolzene Butter,
lauwarmes Wasser und 1 EL
Rosenwasser langsam
hinzugeben und zu einem
Teig kneten. Für 12 Stunden
im Kühlschrank ruhen
lassen. — Die Pistazien sehr
fein hacken und mit 100 g
geschmolzener Butter
sowie 2 EL Rosenwasser vermengen. — Aus dem Teig
kleine Bällchen formen.
In die Mitte von jedem Bällchen etwas vom Pistazien-
Butter-Mix hineingeben
und wieder verschließen.
So oft wiederholen, bis der
Teig aufgebraucht ist. Im
vorgeheizten Backofen bei
170°C für 20−25 Minuten
backen, bis die Bällchen
goldbraun gebacken sind.

ZUM ANRICHTEN
Den Puderzucker durch ein
feines Sieb über die Kekse
streuen und mit geraspelten
Pistazien verfeinern.

DOUGH
Mix all dry ingredients
together. Then slowly
add 250 g melted butter,
warm water and 1 Tbsp.
rose water and knead
until you get a soft dough.
Let it rest for at least
12 hours in the fridge.
— Smash the pistachios
with 100 gbutter and
add 2 Tbsp. rose water.
— Get the dough
out of the fridge, form
small balls, and put
approx. 1 tsp. of the
pistachio mix into the
center of each ball
and close it. Repeat
until all dough is used.
— Bake the balls in a
preheated oven at 170 °C
for 20−25 minutes
until the balls are golden.

FOR SERVING
Sprinkle the icing
sugar through a sieve
over the biscuits
and refine with grated
pistachios.

STICHWÖRTERVERZEICHNIS INDEX

AFFENBROTBAUMGEWÜRZ

Der afrikanische Affenbrotbaum bzw. Baobab gehört zu
den bekanntesten Bäumen
des tropischen Afrikas. Sein
Name leitet sich aus dem
arabischen Begriff „bu hibab"
ab – Frucht mit vielen Samen. Im unbelaubten Zu-
stand erinnert die Astkrone
des Baobab an ein viel
verzweigtes Wurzelsystem,
was zu der sehr verbreiteten
Legende beigetragen hat,
der Affenbrotbaum sei ein
vom Teufel verkehrt herum
gepflanzter Baum.

Die großen Baobab-Blüten
sind weiß und hängen an langen Stielen herab. Während
der Nacht werden die Blüten
vor allem durch Flughunde
bestäubt. Danach entwickeln
sich an den langen Stielen
Kapseln, in denen sich die
Samen befinden. Diese werden u.a. geröstet gegessen
oder fermentiert als Gewürz
verwendet.

GETROCKNETE
LIMETTEN
DRIED LIMES

BAOBAB

The African baobab is one
of tropical Africa's best
known trees. Its name de-
rives from the Arabic term
"bu hibab"- fruit with many
seeds. In its leafless state,
its crown is reminiscent of
an extensively branched root
system, which has contri-
buted to the popular legend
that the devil planted the
tree upside down.

The large baobab flowers
are white and hang on long
stalks. During the night
they are pollinated mainly
by fruit bats. After polli-
nation, seed pods develop
on the long stems, which
contain the seeds. These
are eaten roasted, or fer-
mented and used as a spice.

AJÍ AMARILLO

In Südamerika werden Chili-
schoten als „ají" bezeichnet;
die gelbe Chilischote bzw.
„ají amarillo" stellt dabei
eine mildere Variante dar, die
länglichen Schoten sind
noch nicht zu ihrer orange-
roten Farbe ausgereift. Eine
Paste aus ají amarillo ist
eine Grundzutat etwa der
peruanischen Küche. Dafür
werden die Schoten kurz
in kochendem Wasser
blanchiert, geschält und
püriert. Die leuchtend
gelbe Paste kann eingefroren werden.

AFFENBROTBAUM
BAOBAB

AJI AMARILLO

In South America, chilis are
known as "ají". Yellow chilis, or "ají amarillo", represent
a milder type. The oblong
shaped chilis have not yet
ripened to their orange color.
A paste made from "ají amarillo" is a basic ingredient
of Peruvian cuisine. The yellow chilis are blanched briefly in boiling water, peeled
and pureed. The glowing yellow paste can be deep frozen.

ARABISCHES
SIEBENGEWÜRZ

Beim Arabischen Siebenge-
würz handelt es sich um eine
Gewürzmischung, die sich
im Wesentlichen auf sieben
Zutaten beschränkt. Die Zahl
7 ist im Islam eine Glücks-
zahl. Je nach Region kann die
Zusammenstellung der Ge-
würze variieren. Zumeist wird
die Mischung aus Piment,
Zimt, Koriander, Nelken,
Muskatnuss, Kardamom und

204

Cumin hergestellt. Die Kombination von starkem Zimt-, Nelken- und Pimentaroma ist sehr typisch für die orientalische Küche. Siebengewürze eignen sich besonders für Reis- und Hackfleischgerichte und können Füllungen, Gemüse, Eintöpfe oder Suppen sehr schmackhaft aufwerten.

ARABIC SEVEN SPICES
Arabic seven spices is a spice mixture that is substantially limited to seven ingredients. The number 7 is a lucky number in Islam. Depending on the region, the assortment of spices can vary but mostly the mixture contains allspice, cinnamon, coriander, cloves, nutmeg, cardamom and cumin. The combination of the strong flavors of cinnamon, clove and allspice is very typical for the oriental cuisine. Seven spices are particularly suitable for rice and meat dishes and can elevate fillings, vegetables, stews or soups.

ÉTOUFFÉE-TAUBE
Étouffée-Tauben oder sogenannte Bluttauben wurden erdrosselt und nicht geschlachtet. Das Blut verbleibt dabei im Muskelgewebe und das Fleisch ist entsprechend röter, zarter und schmackhafter.

ÉTOUFFÉE PIGEON
Étouffée pigeons or so-called bloodstewed pigeons were strangled and not slaughtered. The blood remains in the muscle tissue and the meat is accordingly redder, more tender and tastier.

GETROCKNETE GRANATAPFELKERNE
Frische Granatapfelkerne werden als fruchtiger Bestandteil von Salaten, Desserts und Hauptgerichten gerne verwendet. Weniger bekannt ist die Verwendung von getrockneten Kernen in der arabischen Küche. Wenn sich die Saison der Granatäpfel mit dem Winter dem Ende neigt, können die getrockneten Kerne ganz oder gemahlen für eine milde Säure eingesetzt werden.

DRIED POMEGRANATE SEEDS
Fresh pomegranate seeds are used as a fruity component of salads, desserts and main dishes. Lesser known is the use of the dried seeds in Arabic cooking. When the pomegranate season comes to an end in Winter, the dried seeds can be used, either whole or ground, to add a mildly acidic taste.

GHEE
Ghee ist das vor allem in Indien und Pakistan verbreitete Butterschmalz. Es handelt sich dabei um geklärte Butter, die im Gegensatz zum herkömmlichen, in Deutschland verbreiteten Butterschmalz nur noch das reine Fett der Butter enthält. Eiweiß, Milchzucker und Wasser der Butter werden durch Köcheln vom Fett getrennt. Dadurch ist Ghee auch deutlich länger haltbar als normale Butter. Außerdem kann Ghee höher erhitzt werden als Butter und Butterschmalz und hat ein nussiges Aroma.

GHEE
Ghee is a version of clarified butter used mainly in India and Pakistan. It is clarified butter, which, in contrast to the commonly used butter in Germany, contains only the pure fat of the butter. Through simmering, protein, lactose and water from the butter are separated from the fat. This makes ghee last longer than normal butter. Additionally, ghee can be heated to higher temperatures than butter and gains a nutty aroma.

LABNEH
Labneh ist eine Art Frischkäse aus Joghurt. Die Molke wird dem Joghurt entzogen, der dadurch einen leicht

salzigen, cremigen Charakter mit einer feinen Säure erhält. Labneh ist vor allem in Nordafrika, dem Nahen Osten und im Iran verbreitet.

LABNEH

Labneh is a kind of cream cheese made from yoghurt. The whey is being extracted from the yoghurt, which thereby receives a slightly salty, creamy character with a fine acidity. Labneh is mainly prevalent in North Africa, the Middle East and in Iran.

LIMETTEN, GETROCKNETE

Getrocknete Limetten, auch Loomi genannt, sind eine in der orientalischen Küche häufig verwendete Zutat. Die erst in Salzwasser gekochten Limetten werden anschließend in der Sonne getrocknet und erlangen so ihren einzigartigen Geschmack. Als Würzmittel werden getrocknete Limetten meist in langschmorenden Eintöpfen oder Reisgerichten verwendet. Sie ver-

OKRA

GHEE

leihen den Gerichten einen strengen Zitrusduft und ein erfrischend säuerliches Aroma.

LIMES, DRIED

Dried limes, also called Loomi, are commonly used in oriental cuisine. The limes gain their unique taste after being cooked in salt water and then being dried in the sun.

As a spice, dried limes are mostly used in stews or rice dishes. They give the dishes a strict citrus scent and a refreshing sour taste.

OKRA

Okra, auch quiabo (Brasilien), bhindi (Südasien), quimbombó (Kuba) und ba-

OKRA

Okra, also known as quiabo (Brazil), bhindi (South Asia), quimbombó (Cuba), and

mya (u.a. in den arabischen Ländern) genannt, ist eine ursprünglich aus dem Hochland Äthiopiens stammende Gemüsepflanze. Okraschoten sind damit eine der ältesten Gemüsepflanzen weltweit. Beim Kochen sondern die Schoten eine schleimige Flüssigkeit ab, die sich zum Eindicken der Speisen eignet. Entweder durch kurzes Blanchieren in Essigwasser oder durch scharfes Anbraten in Speiseöl kann dieser Effekt jedoch bei Bedarf einfach vermieden werden.

bamya (e.g. in Arabic countries), is a vegetable originally from the highlands of Ethiopia. The green okras are one of the world's oldest vegetables. During cooking the pods release a slimy liquid, which is suitable for thickening sauces. However, this effect can easily be avoided by either blanching in vinegar or searing in oil.

ROSENWASSER

Rosenwasser ist in der arabischen Küche sehr beliebt und trägt zur Aromatisierung von Speisen bei. Bei der Destillation von Rosenöl entsteht das ätherische Wasser als Nebenprodukt. Vor allem auf Milch basierende Nachspeisen kann Rosenwasser um eine feine Geschmacksnote erweitern.

ROSE WATER

Rose water is a favorite in the Arabic cuisine and is used to lend aroma to dishes. The essential water is a by-product of the distillation of rose oil. Rose water can add a fine aromatic taste, especially to milk-based desserts.

SUMAK

Der Gewürz-Sumak oder Sumach bzw. Färberbaum ist ein kleiner Baum, der u.a. in Sizilien, dem Iran und der Türkei auch als Wildpflanze vorkommt. Die Steinfrüchte der Pflanze werden getrocknet, gemahlen und als säuerliches Gewürz vor allem in der türkischen, arabischen, kurdischen und persischen Küche verwendet. Die Verwendung von Sumak ist schon für die Antike nachgewiesen. Sumak kann als Ersatz für Zitronensaft verwendet werden.

SUMAC
Rhus coriaria, a small tree from which the spice sumac is derived, grows in Sicily, Iran and Turkey, amongst other places. The fruits of the plant are dried and ground and used as a bitter spice, mainly in the Turkish, Arabic, Kurdish and Persian cuisines. The use of sumac can be traced back to antiquity. Sumac can be used as an alternative to lemon juice.

TAHINA
Die Tahina, eine feine und helle Paste aus Sesamkörnern, findet sich in jedem türkischen oder arabischen Supermarkt. Sie ist eine grundlegende Zutat für Gerichte wie das Kichererbsenmus Hummus. Mit Zitronensaft, Knoblauch und Sumak verfeinert, kann die Paste auch als Dip gereicht werden.

TAHINI
Tahini, a fine, light colored paste made from sesame seeds, can be found in any Turkish or Arabic supermar-

ket. It is a basic ingredient of dishes like hummus. Used with lemon juice, garlic and sumac, the paste can also be used as a dip.

TAPIOKA
Als Tapioka wird meist ein Granulat bezeichnet, das aus getrockneten Maniok- oder Kassava-Wurzeln gewonnen wird. Für die Weiterverwendung muss Tapioka mit Wasser eingeweicht oder nass verarbeitet werden. Das Wort „Tapioka" hat seinen etymologischen Ur-

sprung in der Tupi-Sprache und damit in den indigenen Kulturen Brasiliens bzw. Südamerikas. In Brasilien wird aus dem Tapiokamehl hauptsächlich eine Art Pfannkuchen mit verschiedenen Füllungen hergestellt. Von Asien aus hat der Bubble Tea mit Tapioka-Kugeln die ganze Welt erobert.

TAPIOCA
Tapioca is the name for a granule which is obtained from the roots of dried manioc or cassava. The

tapioca must be softened by soaking in water or used damp. The word tapioca has its etymological origins in the Tupi language and the indigenous culture of Brazil and South America. In Brazil the tapioca flour is used mainly to make pancakes with various fillings. From Asia, bubble tea containing balls of tapioca has conquered the world.

WILDKRÄUTER
Die frischen Triebe und jungen Blätter von heimischen Wildkräutern wie Schafgarbe, Sauerklee und Wiesenkerbel bereichern die deutsche Küche in Frühling und Sommer. Frische Küchenkräuter haben eine ausgezeichnete und dabei doch milde Würzkraft. Während diese Kräuter bis ins 17. Jahrhundert vor allem als Heilpflanzen bekannt waren, so werden sie heute vor allem wegen ihrer kulinarischen Fähigkeiten z.B. für Salate und Gemüsegerichte genutzt.

WILD HERBS
The fresh stems and young leaves of indigenous herbs like yarrow, sorrel and cow enrich the German cuisine in spring and summer. Fresh herbs have a distinct and yet mild flavor. While these herbs were known in the 17th century primarily as medicinal plants, nowadays they have mainly culinary uses, in salads and vegetable dishes.

GETROCKNETE GRANATAPFELKERNE
DRIED POMEGRANATE SEEDS

VORSTELLUNG DER KÖCHE MEET THE COOKS

LINKS MICHAEL KEMPF
RECHTS REZA AHMADI

ANDREAS TUFFENTSAMMER
Herkunft: Oberdorf am Ipf, Deutschland
Komm mich besuchen:
www.andreastuffentsammer.de
Origin: Oberdorf am Ipf, Germany
Visit me: www.andreastuffentsammer.de

MUDAR EL SHEICH AHMAD
Herkunft: Aleppo, Syrien
Komm mich besuchen: Kitchen Hub,
Roßbachstraße 6, 10829 Berlin
Origin: Aleppo, Syria
Visit me: Kitchen Hub,
Roßbachstraße 6, 10829 Berlin

MICHAEL KEMPF
Herkunft: Sigmaringen, Deutschland
Komm mich besuchen: FACIL,
Potsdamer Straße 3, 10785 Berlin
Origin: Sigmaringen, Germany
Visit me: FACIL, Potsdamer Straße 3,
10785 Berlin

REZA AHMADI
Herkunft: Herat, Afghanistan
Komm mich besuchen: Kitchen Hub,
Roßbachstraße 6, 10829 Berlin
Origin: Herat, Afghanistan
Visit me: Kitchen Hub,
Roßbachstraße 6, 10829 Berlin

ANDREAS TUFFENTSAMMER LINKS
MUDAR EL SHEICH AHMAD RECHTS

3

MUSTAPHA MANNEH LINKS
HOLGER ZURBRÜGGEN RECHTS

MUSTAPHA MANNEH
Herkunft: Mandinari, Gambia
Komm mich besuchen: Bantabaa e.V.,
Falckensteinstraße 18, 10997 Berlin
Origin: Mandinari, Gambia
Visit me: Bantabaa e.V.,
Falckensteinstraße 18, 10997 Berlin

HOLGER ZURBRÜGGEN
Herkunft: Greven, Deutschland
Komm mich besuchen: Balthazar &
Balthazar2, Kurfürstendamm 106,
10711 Berlin & Spreeufer 2, 10178 Berlin
Origin: Greven, Germany
Visit me: Balthazar & Balthazar2,
Kurfürstendamm 106, 10711 Berlin &
Spreeufer 2, 10178 Berlin

ALAA ABU HASHEM
Herkunft: Aleppo, Syrien
Komm mich besuchen: Kitchen Hub,
Roßbachstraße 6, 10829 Berlin
Origin: Aleppo, Syria
Visit me: Kitchen Hub,
Roßbachstraße 6, 10829 Berlin

RALF ZACHERL
Herkunft: Wertheim, Deutschland
Komm mich besuchen: SchmidtZ&KO,
Rheinstraße 45–46, 12161 Berlin
Origin: Wertheim, Germany
Visit me: SchmidtZ&KO,
Rheinstraße 45–46, 12161 Berlin

4

ALAA ABU HASHEM LINKS
RALF ZACHERL RECHTS

SEBASTIAN FRANK LINKS
WAJID ALI RECHTS

5

SEBASTIAN FRANK
Herkunft: Mödling, Österreich
Komm mich besuchen: Restaurant Horváth,
Paul-Lincke-Ufer 44a, 10999 Berlin
Origin: Mödling, Austria
Visit me: Restaurant Horváth,
Paul-Lincke-Ufer 44a, 10999 Berlin

WAJID ALI
Herkunft: Rawalpindi, Pakistan
Komm mich besuchen: Kitchen Hub,
Roßbachstraße 6, 10829 Berlin
Origin: Rawalpindi, Pakistan
Visit me: Kitchen Hub,
Roßbachstraße 6, 10829 Berlin

SARA CHIHABI
Herkunft: Damaskus, Syrien
Komm mich besuchen: Kitchen Hub,
Roßbachstraße 6, 10829 Berlin
Origin: Damaskus, Syria
Visit me: Kitchen Hub,
Roßbachstraße 6, 10829 Berlin

SABINE HUECK
Herkunft: São Paulo, Brasilien
Komm mich besuchen:
Sabine Hueck - Atelier Culinário,
Kyffhäuser Straße 21, 10781 Berlin
Origin: São Paulo, Brazil
Visit me: Sabine Hueck - Atelier Culinário,
Kyffhäuser Straße 21, 10781 Berlin

SIMI ANAND LINKS
DIEGO MUÑOZ RECHTS

SIMI ANAND
Herkunft: Herat, Afghanistan
Komm mich besuchen: Kitchen Hub,
Roßbachstraße 6, 10829 Berlin
Origin: Herat, Afghanistan
Visit me: Kitchen Hub,
Roßbachstraße 6, 10829 Berlin

DIEGO MUÑOZ
Herkunft: Lima, Peru
Komm mich besuchen: Astrid y Gastón,
Av. Paz Soldán 290,
San Isidro, Lima 27 - Perú
Origin: Lima, Peru
Visit me: Astrid y Gastón,
Av. Paz Soldán 290,
San Isidro, Lima 27 - Perú

SARA CHIHABI LINKS
SABINE HUECK RECHTS

6

SVEN ELVERFELD LINKS
GHAITH HANKI RECHTS

MZKIN MATINI
Herkunft: Damaskus, Syrien
Komm mich besuchen: Kitchen Hub,
Roßbachstraße 6, 10829 Berlin
Origin: Damaskus, Syria
Visit me: Kitchen Hub,
Roßbachstraße 6, 10829 Berlin

WILFRIED BANCQUART
Herkunft: Dunkerque, Frankreich
Komm mich besuchen:
Französische Botschaft in Berlin,
Pariser Platz 5, 10117 Berlin
Origin: Dunkerque, France
Visit me: French Embassy in Berlin,
Pariser Platz 5, 10117 Berlin

SVEN ELVERFELD
Herkunft: Hanau, Deutschland
Komm mich besuchen: Aqua,
Parkstraße 1, 38440 Wolfsburg
Origin: Hanau, Germany
Visit me: Aqua, Parkstraße 1,
38440 Wolfsburg

GHAITH HANKI
Herkunft: Aleppo, Syrien
Komm mich besuchen: Kitchen Hub,
Roßbachstraße 6, 10829 Berlin
Origin: Aleppo, Syria
Visit me: Kitchen Hub,
Roßbachstraße 6, 10829 Berlin

MZKIN MATINI LINKS
WILFRIED BANCQUART RECHTS

MOUHAMED TANKO LINKS
MATHIAS SAUTER RECHTS

10

MOUHAMED TANKO
Herkunft: Maradi, Niger
Komm mich besuchen: Kitchen Hub,
Roßbachstraße 6, 10829 Berlin
Origin: Maradi, Niger
Visit me: Kitchen Hub,
Roßbachstraße 6, 10829 Berlin

MATHIAS SAUTER
Herkunft: Eisenharz, Deutschland
Komm mich besuchen: Kitchen Hub,
Roßbachstraße 6, 10829 Berlin
Origin: Eisenharz, Germany
Visit me: Kitchen Hub,
Roßbachstraße 6, 10829 Berlin

MALLAKE JAZMATI LINKS
MICHA SCHÄFER RECHTS

11

MALLAKE JAZMATI
Herkunft: Damaskus, Syrien
Komm mich besuchen:
Levante Gourmet Catering,
levante.gourmet@gmail.com
Origin: Damaskus, Syria
Visit me: Levante Gourmet Catering,
levante.gourmet@gmail.com

MICHA SCHÄFER
Herkunft: Unterseen, Schweiz
Komm mich besuchen:
Noberlhart & Schmutzig,
Friedrichstraße 218, 10969 Berlin
Origin: Unterseen, Switzerland
Visit me: Noberlhart & Schmutzig,
Friedrichstraße 218, 10969 Berlin

13

AHMED KOTB
Herkunft: Kairo, Ägypten
Komm mich besuchen: Kitchen Hub,
Roßbachstraße 6, 10829 Berlin
Origin: Cairo, Egypt
Visit me: Kitchen Hub,
Roßbachstraße 6, 10829 Berlin

HARALD HÖLLRIGL
Herkunft: Österreich
Komm mich besuchen: Culinarium Catering,
Prenzlauer Allee 36, 10405 Berlin
Origin: Austria
Visit me: Culinarium Catering,
Prenzlauer Allee 36, 10405 Berlin

AHMED KOTB LINKS
HARALD HÖLLRIGLI RECHTS

12

HADI NSREENY
Herkunft: Aleppo, Syrien
Komm mich besuchen: Wollf & Eber,
Kulmbacher Straße 15, 10777 Berlin
Origin: Aleppo, Syria
Visit me: Wollf & Eber,
Kulmbacher Straße 15, 10777 Berlin

REZEPTAUFLISTUNG

LIST OF RECIPIES

DANKSAGUNG

Es ist uns eine große Freude, das vorliegende Kochbuch zu präsentieren. Mit der Unterstützung einer großen Anzahl von geflüchteten Kochbegeisterten und Sterneköchen, Fotografinnen, Grafikerinnen, Food Stylistinnen und nicht zuletzt dank des unermüdlichen Engagements der Mitarbeitenden und Freiwilligen von *Über den Tellerrand* ist es uns gelungen, ein wundervolles Buch voller Begegnungen und spannender Rezepte zusammenzustellen. Auch die Metro Cash & Carry Deutschland GmbH, die uns mit allen nötigen Lebensmitteln versorgt hat, darf hier nicht unerwähnt bleiben. Wir möchten uns ausdrücklich und von ganzem Herzen bei allen bedanken, die mitgemacht haben. Für ihre Zeit, ihren Einsatz, ihre Ideen, Arbeit und Geschmäcker. Mit fast allen von Euch haben wir schon gemeinsam gekocht und gegessen. Ihr macht unseren Kitchen Hub, das Zuhause von *Über den Tellerrand* mitten auf der Roten Insel in Berlin-Schöneberg, zu diesem magischen Ort voller Kulinarik und Begegnung. Danke.

Den folgenden Personen möchten wir namentlich für Ihre unermüdliche Mitarbeit an diesem Buchprojekt danken:

CARINA ADAM

Carina hat ein ganz besonderes Auge für die Schönheit von Menschen und Essen. Mit viel Liebe, Energie und Kraft hat sie die einzigartigsten Momente jedes Shootings eingefangen und so diesem Buch zu seiner Schönheit verholfen. Danke, Carina!

SABINE HUECK

Besonderer Dank geht an Sabine Hueck und ihr Atelier Culinário. Mit ihrem Charme, ihrer mitreißend positiven Einstellung, ihrer Liebe zum Detail, mit großem Herz und besonderer Kreativität hat sie jede einzelne Kochbegegnung bereichert und das Beste aus jeder Küche, jedem Gericht und jedem Löffel herausgeholt. Danke, Sabine!

DANIA SCHÜÜRMANN

Was wäre ein Buch ohne Worte, die die gelebten Momente, den kulinarischen und persönlichen Austausch so lebhaft wie möglich nacherzählen und den Lesenden so teilhaben lassen an der Entstehungsgeschichte dieses Gemeinschaftswerkes? Nichts. Großer Dank an unsere „Schreibqueen", Dania!

MATHIAS SAUTER

In der Ruhe liegt die Kraft. Dank Mathias' positiver Einstellung, seiner Gelassenheit und zupackenden Art wurden so manche Stress-Momente aufgefangen und in pure Motivation verwandelt. Danke, Mathias!

GRAFIKLADEN

Katharina und Johanna haben keine Kraft und Mühen gescheut, unserem Buch die passende schöne Form zu verleihen. Zwei inspirierende Persönlichkeiten, ohne die „Eine Prise Heimat" nicht das selbe Buch wäre. Danke, Ihr beiden! Danke auch an Shirley, die bei der Auswahl des Covers viele Ideen eingebracht hat.

Nicht zu vergessen auch der Dank an Victoria Hugelshofer und Juliane Pfuhl, die neben den Übersetzungen stets eine Schulter zum Anlehnen boten und ihre bezaubernden Ideen nicht zurückgehalten haben.

Ein riesiges Dankeschön gebührt dem gesamten Team von *Über den Tellerrand*, das die Buch-Crew ertragen hat, immer fleißig und ehrlich Feedback gegeben hat und artig alles aufgegessen hat, was wir während der Buchproduktion an Köstlichkeiten hergestellt haben.

Darüber hinaus wurde unser Verein *Über den Tellerrand e.V.* so weit vorangebracht, dass mittlerweile in 25 Städten über den Tellerrand gekocht wird und sich in unserem Kitchen Hub täglich viele inspirierende Menschen voller Ideen und Motivation tummeln. Esther, Linn, Rafael, Linda, Nicole und Agnes: You rock!

222

ACKNOWLEDGMENTS

It is a great pleasure for us to present this cookbook to you. With the support of an amazing team of enthusiastic refugee chefs, head chefs, photographers, graphic designers, food-stylists and last but not least, the tireless support of our employees and volunteers at *Über den Tellerrand*, we succeeded in putting together this wonderful cookbook full of new encounters and exciting recipes. We would also like to thank the Metro Cash & Carry Deutschland GmbH who supplied us with all necessary ingredients.

We would truly like to thank everybody who contributed to this project. We are extremely grateful for their time, commitment, ideas, work and taste! We prepared and ate delicious dishes with almost all of you, and it was you who turned our Kitchen Hub, home of *Über den Tellerrand*, into this magical place full of discovery and culinary experiences. Thank you.

A special thanks goes to the following persons for their tireless contribution and help with this project:

CARINA ADAM

Carina has a special talent to see the beauty in individual people and in food. With a lot of love, energy and strength she captured the most unique moments of our culinary journey and has made this book as beautiful as it is. Thank you Carina!

SABINE HUECK

We would like to extend a warm thanks to Sabine Hueck and her studio Atelier Culinário.

Her charm and contagiously positive attitude, her attention to detail, her big heart and special creativity has enriched every cooking encounter and made the best out of every kitchen, every dish and every spoon. Thank you Sabine!

DANIA SCHÜÜRMANN

What would a book be without words that can recount all those special moments, and all the culinary and personal exchanges as vividly as possible? A big thank you to our "storytelling queen" Dania, for taking the reader on a journey through our extraordinary collaborative project!

MATHIAS SAUTER

Strength lies in calmness. Thanks to Mathias' positive attitude, his composure and his problem-solving approach: you managed to turn challenges into constructive outcomes through your infallible motivation. Thank you Mathias!

GRAFIKLADEN

Katharina and Johanna spared neither energy nor effort to bring our book into shape. Two inspiring personalities, without whom "A pinch of home" would not be as beautiful as it is! Thank you both!

Thanks also to Shirley, whose advice was very helpful when selecting our book cover.

Last but not least, a huge thanks goes to Victoria Hugelshofer and Juliane Pfuhl, our two talented translators who were always a shoulder to lean on and who never failed to contribute their brilliant ideas to the project.

A huge thank you goes to the entire team from *Über den Tellerrand* which has endured the "book crew" whilst always giving honest feedback and bravely tasting every new dish that has been created for the book.

In addition to that, the team has brought *Über den Tellerrand e.V.* so far since it began: Now, many inspiring and motivated people exchange stories and ideas in our Kitchen Hub in Berlin every day, and we have twenty-five satellite projects around Germany. Esther, Linn, Rafael, Linda, Nicole and Agnes: You rock!

IMPRESSUM

1. Ausgabe, 1. Auflage Berlin 2016
Alle Rechte vorbehalten.

Über den Tellerrand kochen GmbH
Roßbachstraße 6
10829 Berlin

www.ueberdentellerrand.org

PROJEKTLEITUNG
Lisa Thaens

TEXTBEARBEITUNG
Dania Schüürmann
Juliane Pfuhl
Victoria Hugelshofer
Steffi Demetry
Laurenz Schaller

FOTOGRAFIE UND
BILDBEARBEITUNG
Carina Adam
www.carinaadam.com

SETSTYLING
Sabine Hueck - Atelier Culinário
www.sabinehueck.de

GESTALTUNG
Grafikladen Berlin
www.grafikladen.net

DRUCK UND
BUCHBINDERISCHE
VERARBEITUNG
Firmengruppe APPL
aprinta GmbH

VETRIEBSPARTNER
Münchener Verlagsgruppe GmbH

ISBN: 978-3-86883-606-6